WORDS BEYOND THE WOODS

A Tapestry On Arunachala In Verse

Dr M Balaji Prasad

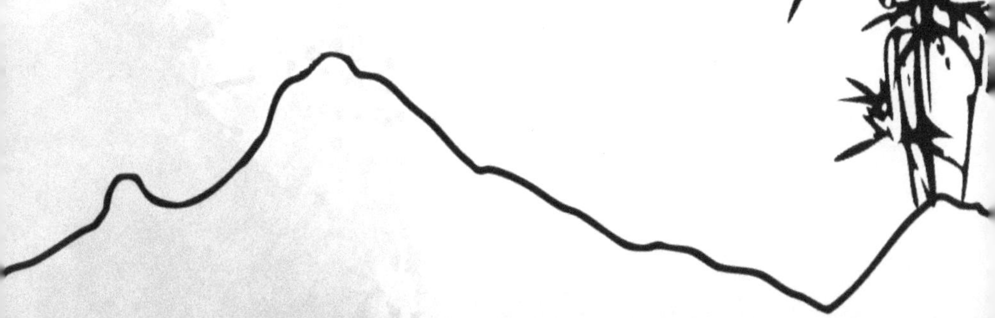

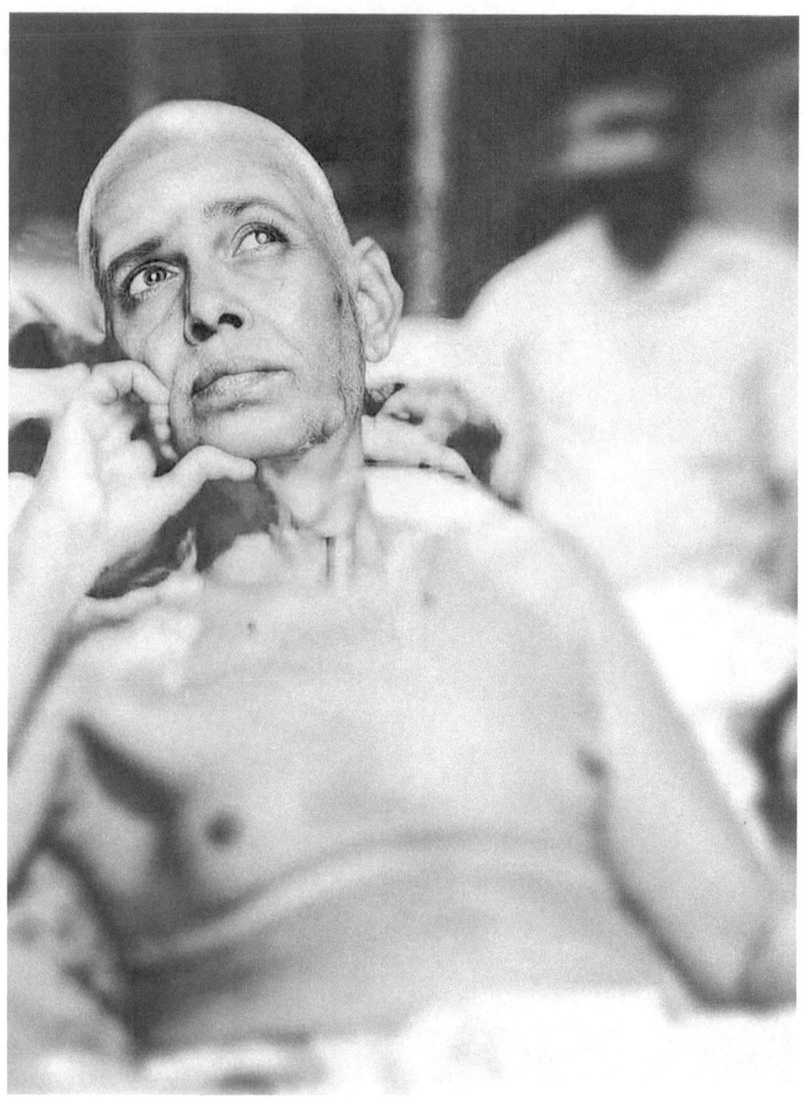

Contents

Contents

A Prologue

Poetry and devotion have frequently been linked throughout history. The bond between poetry and devotion is significant. Poetry acts as a conduit through which profound spiritual emotions can be articulated. The fundamental desire to connect with the divine manifests in lyrical structures that often embody deep emotion. This bond can be traced across various cultures and epochs, underscoring our yearning for a connection beyond the ordinary.

Historically, poetry has been utilized as a means for expressing devotion in different religious traditions. In ancient writings, such as the Vedas in Hinduism and biblical psalms in Judaism and Christianity, poetic forms that convey reverence, praise, and supplication are evident. In a similar vein, the Islamic Sufi tradition experienced the emergence of poets like Rumi, whose writings are celebrated for their mystical profundity and lyrical charm. Rumi's poetry goes beyond the limitations of religious doctrines, employing compelling imagery of love and yearning to express the desire for unity with the divine. These early illustrations demonstrate how poetry is naturally suited to the articulation of transcendent experiences.

The inherent features of poetry - its talent for striking imagery, musical qualities, and emotional power - render it an especially effective medium for articulating the intricacies of religious belief. The brief and frequently symbolic terminology of poetry reflects the mystical and often indescribable essence of spiritual experience. Within the Hindu tradition, devotional poetry, known as bhakti poetry, thrived for centuries. The creations of Kabir, a mystic poet from the 15th century, blended Sufi and Hindu influences, using straightforward, relatable language to convey profound spiritual insights. His poems frequently included metaphors drawn from everyday experiences, making his devotional themes accessible to a broad audience. These poets exemplified the ability of poetry to connect the human experience with the divine realm.

Tamil poetry has historically been a lively and essential aspect of Tamil culture. Its connection with spirituality, provides an intense examination of the human experience, communal consciousness, and the divine. The core of Tamil poetry can be traced back to ancient literature, where themes of love, nature, and spirituality are interwoven. The Sangam literature, one of the earliest compilations of Tamil poetry, established the groundwork for this connection. The poets from the Sangam period portrayed not only the fertile landscapes of Tamil Nadu but also the philosophical and spiritual issues concerning humanity. The verses from these ancient texts reveal a profound bond between nature and the divine, illustrating a universe where spirituality manifests through the allure of both the tangible and the intangible.

It is impossible to discuss Tamil poetry without recognizing the substantial impact of the Tamil Siddhas. These mystical poets and sages, who were active during the medieval era, fused spiritual practice with poetic expression. Their works often explore themes of self-realization, divine love, and the pursuit of enlightenment.

The Bhakti movement in Tamil Nadu further influenced the spiritual terrain of Tamil poetry. Saints like Alvars and Nayanmars concentrated on the devotion to personal deities, highlighting a direct and personal relationship with the divine. Their poetry featured vivid expressions of love and longing, encapsulating the essence of spiritual devotion. This movement made spirituality more accessible, encouraging individuals, regardless of caste or position, to pursue a personal connection with the divine. Their verses represent more than just religious poetry; they are reflections of profound yearning for unity with God, showcasing how love surpasses societal boundaries.

One vital component of the spiritual connection in Tamil poetry is its musicality. The phonetic charm of the Tamil language enhances the poetic experience, enabling spiritual topics to resonate emotionally with both readers and listeners. Numerous contemporary poets are also lyricists, further merging the boundaries between poetry and music. This intersection opens up new pathways for spiritual expression that reach broader audiences, making spirituality relatable and accessible through mainstream culture.

Different perspectives exist regarding the function of poetry in devotion. One perspective posits that poetry can serve as a bridge between the individual and the divine. It transforms personal experiences into a collective language that nurtures the community. Through communal reading, recitation, and interpretation, the devotional aspect of poetry can bolster a sense of belonging within a faithful community. Furthermore, poetry can provide comfort during crises. The written word can serve as a source of solace, articulating emotions that are often challenging to convey.

A Journey of Spiritual Exploration

The essence of the book, Words Beyond the Woods, lies in its ability to guide readers through the spiritual quests that have long been associated with Arunachala. Dr. Prasad's verses encapsulate the ethereal beauty of the sacred mountain while delving into the depths of human consciousness and the quest for truth. The poetic structure of the book invites readers to reflect deeply on their spiritual journeys, making it a meditative experience.

Through rich imagery and evocative language, the author captures the essence of the natural surroundings and the mystical aura of Arunachala. Each verse serves as a stepping stone towards understanding the profound spiritual truths that the mountain symbolizes. This exploration of the sacred landscape is not only geographical but also metaphysical, as it encourages readers to look inward and seek the divine within themselves.

The Influence of Sri Ramana Maharshi

A significant highlight of this book is Dr. Prasad's emphasis on Sri Ramana Maharshi, a luminary figure in Indian spirituality. The Maharshi's teachings on self-inquiry and the nature of the self are interwoven throughout the verses, offering readers insights into his profound philosophy.

The author deftly illustrates how Sri Ramana Maharshi's life and teachings resonate with the essence of Arunachala, making the mountain not just a physical space but a spiritual beacon. Dr. Prasad captures the Maharshi's teachings with clarity and reverence, making them accessible to both seasoned spiritual seekers and those new to his philosophy. The inclusion of

Maharshi's concepts serves to deepen the reader's understanding of self-realization and the journey towards inner peace.

In conclusion, Words Beyond the Woods - A Tapestry on Arunachala in Verse by Dr. M Balaji Prasad is a remarkable contribution to spiritual literature. It offers readers a unique blend of poetic beauty and philosophical depth, inviting them to embark on their journeys of self-discovery. Through the lens of Arunachala and the teachings of Sri Ramana Maharshi, the book stands as a testament to the enduring quest for meaning and enlightenment in the human experience. This work is a must-read for anyone seeking to deepen their understanding of spirituality and the sacredness of self-realization.

Acknowledgement

I would like to express my heartfelt gratitude to Dr. Anand Ramanan, The President of Sri Ramanasramam, The Agshiv Photography, Mr. Reinhard Jung, Mr. Bernd Kalidas Flory, Mr. Aaruran and Mr. Markus Horlacher for kindly allowing me to use the photos of Bhagavan Sri Ramana Maharshi and Sacred Arunachala. This permission means a lot to me, as it connects my words to the deep wisdom and teachings of Maharshi. His peaceful presence in the images adds beauty and inspiration to my poetry. I am truly thankful to all for their support, which brings a sense of spiritual depth to my work.

The Primordial Hum: Echoes of OM

Before the first rays shone,
Before the universe was called into existence,
A sound existed, quiet, profound, and immense,
The origin of all, spanning from the future to the past.
The ancient Hum, an intense vibration,
From which all energies and forms originated.

No words could mould it, no ear could fully grasp it,
Yet in its nature, all cherished things reside.
The breath of Brahma, crafting unseen worlds,
A cosmic whisper, eternally tranquil.
The Om emerged, the hallowed syllable,
The universe's initial and endless thrill.

It resonates in the rustling leaves,
The crashing waves and the wind that weaves
Through mountain heights, a gentle yet powerful sound,
The essential note to which we are all connected.
A resonance that ties together stars and dust,
An inherent truth, arising from pure trust.

Within each heart, a resonant melody,
A persistent beat that soothes all pain.
A mantra softly spoken, alleviating every fear,

An inward journey, clarifying the spirit.
In meditation's tranquillity, we can discover,
The primal Hum within the seeking mind.

It is the silence that embraces every sound,
The blank canvas on which all forms appear.
The beginning and the end, intertwined,
A unity that leaves no soul excluded.
In every atom, across the vast universe,
The Primordial Hum dances in its cosmic rhythm.

2

Source of Wisdom:
An Epic Invocation to Gajanana

Before the peak of the fire, Arunachala's might,
Before the verses bloom in sacred light,
I turn to Him, the Lord of Auspicious Start,
Gajanana enthroned within the heart.

O form of wisdom, with thy gentle hand,
That holds the lotus, granting every demand,
Thy tusk, a scribe of ancient, holy lore,
Now guide this pen to open Arunachala's door.

Thou art the remover, Vignaharta bold,
Whose mighty trunk the tangled paths unfold.
Let no obstruction hinder now my quest,
To capture the beauty on that mountain blessed.

Bestow thy insight, Buddhipriya bright,
Illumine thoughts with Arunachala's light.
Inspire the rhythm, let the verses flow,
Like the sacred Ganga, from the mountain's snow.

O Lambodara, with thy generous grace,
Embrace this effort in thy vast embrace.
Grant me the words to paint the vibrant scene,
Where earthly meets the realm that lies unseen.

So, hear my call, O Ganesha divine,
Before these poems on Arunachala shine.
Bless every stanza, every line I write,
And fill my verses with thy sacred light!

Om Gam Ganapataye Namaha!
May my words take flight!

3

In the Light of Silence: A Tribute to Sri Ramana Maharshi

In the hallowed hills along Tiruvannamalai's shore,
A sage roamed, endowed with profound knowledge.
Ramana Maharshi, a name held in deep regard,
A guide to innumerable souls, with an unwavering heart.

His gaze twinkled like stars in the night,
Emitting kindness, sparking a light.
He saw beyond illusions, reaching the essence,
Guiding seekers to their innermost presence.

Born in eighteen seventy-nine,
An unremarkable child, yet soon to brightly shine.
He left home, seeking peaks so grand,
In quest of truth, before dawn could expand.

At seventeen, he reached Arunachala's foot,
Where he sat in peace, in a serene pursuit.
The mountain's spirit ignited his inner flame,
A light that flourished, illuminating the same.

For years he pondered, engulfed in profound calm,
His mind serene, like quiet waters that balm.
The outside world faded, like an echoing chime,
As he delved deeper into the Self's sacred climb.

He unveiled the way, to the inquiry "Who Am I?" so profound,
A journey that leads to the Self newly found.
"Simply be yourself," he counselled with gentle mirth,
"No need to chase, just embrace your worth."

His insights spread far and wide, throughout the lovely domain,
A message of empathy, without any strain.
He welcomed all, with open arms and heart,
No distinction made, 'tween the wealthy or the less, each played
their part.

His ashram flourished, a sanctuary for the soul,
Where seekers gathered, both nearby and far, whole.
They brought their queries, about the roads they would roam,
And he replied with wisdom, woven into a tapestry of his own.

The concept of ego, he revealed with a grin,
A mere pretence, that keeps us spinning within.
The fabric of the mind, he portrayed as but a show,
A fleeting dream, that must dissolve, as we learn to grow.

The power of self-inquiry, he demonstrated with grace,
A technique to slice through the ego's tight embrace.
By examining our thoughts, we unveil our true core,
The answers lie within, an infinite store.

As the years swiftly flew, Ramana aged with poise,
His body grew frail, but his spirit retained its voice.
Yet he kept teaching, with words ever glowing,
Until his final breath, in the gentle light flowing.

On April fourteenth, in the span of nineteen fifty,
He closed his eyes, in a serene state, peacefully nifty.
But his legacy lingers, a flame that stays bright,
Continuing to steer us, on paths of spiritual light.

So, let us pay tribute to Ramana, a sage of high regard,
Whose teachings echo, across this sacred yard.
May we learn from him, the art of being free,
A cherished gift to humanity, for eternity.

4

Rivalry of the Divine: Flames of Challenge

From cosmic slumber, a rivalry arose,
A celestial contest, where ego bestow.
A challenge to the Gods, Vishnu and Brahma, so bright,
To gauge the boundless, Shiva's infinite might.

A pillar of fire, a Lingam of flame,
Ascended beyond reach, whispering Shiva's name.
"He who finds the end, the summit or root,"
Declared a voice echoing, beyond dispute.

Vishnu, the preserver, embarked on his quest,
A boar of immense size, putting speed to the test.
He burrowed down deep, through layers of ground,
Seeking the base of the Lingam, profound.

Aeons, he journeyed, with tireless might,
But Shiva's foundation remained out of sight.
Exhausted and humbled, he conceded defeat,
His pride now diminished; his mission incomplete.

Brahma, the creator, with ego ablaze,
Soared upwards on wings, in a sun-drenched haze.
A swan of great power, he soared ever high,
In search of the pinnacle that reached beyond the sky.

He spotted a Ketaki flower, drifting so free,
A witness, he claimed, to victory's decree.
"I've reached the summit," Brahma declared with glee,
A fabricated truth, for all eyes to see.

But Shiva, the omniscient, with cosmic decree,
Revealed the deception, for eternity.
The flower confessed, forced to bear a false claim,
Brahma's ego shattered, consumed by the flame.

Vishnu, in humility, bowed his head,
Admitting his failure, honestly said.
Shiva, pleased with his truth, his humble embrace,
Bestowed upon Vishnu, honour and grace.

Brahma, exposed, for his boastful deceit,
Received a curse solemn, a bitter defeat.
His temples diminished, his worship grew slight,
A lesson for hubris, in celestial light.

The Lingam remained, a symbol so grand,
Of Shiva's immensity, beyond human understanding.
A contest remembered, for ages to be,
Of humility's virtue, and truthful decree.

5

The Wondrous Sight: The Enigma of Ardhanarishwara

In ancient lands where whispers blend,
Amidst the quiet, tales transcend,
A silhouette of grace did rise,
Ardhanarishwara, blending skies.

In the form divine, the two entwined,
Half Shiva fierce, and half combined,
With Parvati's gentle, nurturing face,
A union blessed in cosmic space.

The world beheld this wondrous sight,
A harmony of day and night,
A balance wrought of strength and grace,
In every heart, they found their place.

Through mountains tall and rivers wide,
In the forest deep where shadows hide,
The spirit danced, the essence flowed,
In every creature, love is bestowed.

Oh, ardent lord of wisdom deep,
In meditation, secrets keep,
With crescent moon upon thy brow,
You guide the lost in solemn vow.

Oh, Ardhanarishwara, essence pure,
Symbol of love, hope, demure,
In you, the cycles intertwine,
Of birth, of death, in sacred line.
As nature sways, to rhythms slow,
In every heart where love shall grow,
You teach the world to harmonize,
To seek the truth beyond the lies.

The clouds adorned in sunlit grace,
Reflect the union, bright embrace,
In every heartbeat, every sigh,
The spirit sings, it cannot lie.

Rejoice, O seekers, in the light,
Of duality, pure and bright,
For in our hearts, this truth resides,
In Ardhanarishwarar, love abides.

An epic was sung in lands afar,
Of Shiva's peace and Parvati's star,
Together as one, they rule the night,
In harmony, we find our sight.

6

Mountain Muse:
Inspiration from Granite Heights

Arunachala, mountain of might,
Thy granite slopes pierce the azure light,
A holy summit, where silence reigns,
And time-worn wisdom silently speaks.

Thy shaded glens, deep and green,
Hold secrets whispered, seldom heard,
Of sages meditating, calm and still,
Upon thy slopes, their souls to fill.

Thy sun-lit apex, rising high,
A beacon gleaming against the sky,
A sacred place, a tranquil scene,
Where peace is profound, forever keen.

Oh, Arunachala, grand and old,
Thy story in the ages told,
Of pilgrims drawn, from far and near,
To seek their solace and cast out fear.

Thy everlasting presence, enduring strength,
A sacred melody, a murmur of hope,
A mountain blessed, a luminous essence.
Arunachala enveloped in brilliance.

7

Valleys of Vision: Where Faith Takes Flight

The Lord of Aruna, a mountain's embrace,
Annamalaiyar, with a sun-kissed face,
A deity ancient, in legend enshrined,
His power is unmatched, his grace you will find.

For ages untold, his story unfolds,
A tale of devotion, courage, and holds,
Of sages and saints, their penance and plea,
To witness his glory, eternally free.

In the heart of the South, where the mountains arise,
His temple stands tall, touching the skies,
A fortress of faith, a beacon of light,
Guiding lost souls through the darkest of nights.

Agni, the fire god, his fierce power displays,
In Annamalai's heart, a celestial blaze,
A symbol of strength, a burning desire,
To cleanse and to purify, raise ever higher.

Arunagirinathar, the poet divine,
Sang hymns of praise, in verses that shine,
His fervent devotion, a passionate plea,
To unravel the secrets, for all men to feel.

Through forests deep, and valleys below,
The pilgrim's journey, their faith brightly aglow,
To reach the sacred peak, with hearts full of grace,
To bask in his presence, find solace and peace.

The lingam, the symbol, of power untold,
A mystical essence, a story unfolds,
Of Shiva's presence, a radiant might,
Illuminating darkness, dispelling the night.

From dawn till dusk, the chants softly rise,
A symphony sacred, that pierces the skies,
The bells gently chime, a sweet, holy sound,
As devotees gather on sacred ground.

The Girivalam path, a journey of might,
Circling the mountain, bathed in holy light,
A pilgrimage arduous, a test of the soul,
To strengthen the spirit, and make it whole.

Through sun-scorched plains, and lakes so deep,
The faithful proceed, their promises to keep,
With every step taken, a prayer softly said,
For blessings and guidance, and strength to be led.

Through trials and tribulations, the spirit takes flight,
Annamalaiyar's presence, a beacon of light,
His love is ever-present, a comforting hand,
Guiding the lost souls across this vast land.

The mountain's great silence, a mystical call,
To surrender to divinity, giving your all,
In the stillness profound, the truth finds its way,
To enlighten the spirit and brighten the day.

So come, pilgrims, wanderers, seekers of grace,
To Annamalaiyar's temple, find peace in this place.
Let the sacred vibrations, cleanse your heart's core,
And leave all your worries, forevermore.

8

Goddess Among Us: The Mirror of Unnamulai's Grace

In the heart of Tiruvannamalai, where the rivers entwine,
Stands Unnamulai, a goddess, divine.
Her image framed in the temple's embrace,
Where prayers echo softly, transcending all space.

She, with arms open wide, against evening's hue,
Wears a crown of the moon, dipped in twilight's dew.
Garlands of jasmine adorn her pearl-studded face,
A visage of compassion, a portrait of grace.

Through corridors of stone, carved by ancient hands,
Her stories unfold in the whispers of sands.
Each mural, a tale of devotion and strife,
Of seekers and sages who yearn for her life.

Her altar adorned with bright turmeric dust,
Devotees gather, their hopes wrapped in trust.
With flickering lamps casting shadows of prayers,
They summon her blessings through delicate wares.

The fragrance of incense encircles the air,
A celestial breeze that can lighten all care.
With every chant rising, like waves to the sky,
She listens, she watches, as moments float by.

In saffron and crimson, her sacred attire,
Draped in devotion, igniting a sweet fire.
Her laughter, a melody that dances through the night,
Like the soft rustle of leaves caught in moonlight.

The peepal trees shiver as secrets are told,
Of love and loss, in whispers of old.
Each offering laid at her feet, a pure hymn,
While the stars hold their breath, allowing her to whim.

In silver-threaded clouds, her essence transcends,
A mother, a warrior, where each tale commends.
Through trials endured, her children remain,
Seeking solace and strength in the ebb of the rain.

The temple bells chime like a heartbeat anew,
Resonating hope in the hearts that pursue.
With pots of fresh milk, they gather each year,
In gratitude's banquet, her blessings so dear.

The sound of her footsteps in soft, silent grace,
Bridges valleys and rivers, transcends time and space.
She walks hand in hand with those who have lost,
Through the journeys of sorrow, she gathers the tossed.

Her laughter lingers in the songs of the breeze,
Through gardens of green where the weary find ease.
She nurtures the souls that have wandered away,
Guiding their paths like the dawn of the day.

Each petal that falls carries whispers of dreams,
Of souls intertwined in celestial beams.
Her mirror reflects the world's multitude,
In every compassion, a love that renews.

At dusk, when the stars gleam, eager to peek,
Each shimmering glow shouts the truth we all seek.
She paints patterns of light on the canvas of night,
A reminder that shadows are part of the light.

As seasons shift gently, she weaves through the years,
With laughter and courage to guide us through our fears.
Her stories embrace all, both humble and grand,
In the heart of each seeker, she silently stands.

In the flicker of flames, her spirit ignites,
In the depth of our struggles, she fosters our fights.
Within each devotion, her heartbeat can swell,
In the silence of night, her presence can tell.

To the travellers weary, she offers a home,
In gardens of solace, no longer they roam.
With blessing and bounty, she fills every heart,
A sanctuary of grace, where all souls can chart.

As petals unfold in the sun's soft caress,
With love intertwined, she mends every distress.
Each tear that is shed becomes a river of prayers,
Winding through mountains, she brings forth repairs.

Her eyes hold the wisdom of ages long past,
In her gaze, there lies a promise steadfast.
Through every storm weathered, she stands ever near,
An echo of strength, a whisper of cheer.

Beneath her soft gaze, the weary find rest,
In the shelter of love, we discover our quest.
With each bead of the mala, a promise we weave,
Goddess Unnamulai, in whom we believe.

As dawn paints horizons with strokes of pure gold,
Her essence enchants and her stories uphold.
In every creation, her spirit's bestowed,
Through the whispers of time, her legacy flowed.

Each chant is a reminder of the journey we share,
In laughter and sorrow, we draw from her care.
Through generations past, and those yet to be,
She nurtures the land, the forest and the sea.

Let the bells sound her glory, let the river flow forth,
Celebrate her presence in the cycles of birth.
For in each seed scattered, in every high tide,
Lives the spirit of Mother Unnamulai, forever our guide.

9

Ghee-Lit Dreams: A Dance with Shadows

Where the earth rises to embrace the grace of the heavens,
Annamalai stands, a venerable, rocky visage.
A quiet guardian, resting in timeless slumber,
Harbouring ancient secrets, cherished by the faithful.
A mountain sage, adorned in the colours of dawn,
Anticipates the moment when darkness yields.

From its summit, a radiant beacon ignites,
Annamalai Deepam, dispelling the shadows.
A blazing promise, etched across the firmament,
A golden response to a heartfelt yearning.
The flames, nourished by ghee, swirl and leap,
A silent dialect, concealing profound truths.

For countless generations, pilgrims converge,
Attracted by the luminosity that dispels all dread.
Their spirits ignited with a longing, sincere and pure,
To unite with the light and experience renewal.
They recite sacred names, a rhythmic invocation,
Seeking liberation from the constraints of existence.

The mountain reverberates with their passionate calls,
As ashes murmur from the revered soil.
A metamorphosis unfolds in the radiant glow,

Where the ego dissolves in the fiery mist.
Each devotee, a spark within the collective,
Releases their burdens and reclaims their essence.

This light ignites a profound awareness within,
A tranquil silence where true serenity resides.
It conveys a message of unity, transcending form and identity,
A universal truth, an everlasting flame.
Thus, let us behold this sacred vision,
And discover within ourselves, the Light of Annamalai.

Barefoot Blessings: A Circle of Reverence

With humble hearts and feet so bare,
Around the hill, a silent prayer,
The Pradakshina starts with care.

Each step a breath, a whispered plea,
Absorbing grace, eternally,
Beneath the ancient banyan tree.

The sun above, a golden eye,
Watches pilgrims as they ply,
Their devotion reaching high.

Through bustling towns and pathways still,
The sacred energy does fill,
Each heart that walks upon this hill.

The scent of incense, sweet and faint,
A tapestry the senses paint,
As weary souls find no complaint.

The distant chants, a gentle hum,
A calling voice that has become,
A part of all, the overcome.

The rocky slopes, a test of will,
Yet peace descends, the spirit still,
As nature's grandeur starts to thrill.

The returning point, the journey's end,
A sense of wholeness, heaven-sent,
The mountain's grace, a faithful friend.

With lighter steps and minds serene,
The cycle closed, the vision keen,
Arunachala, forever seen.

11

Tiruvannamalai's Tapestry: Weaving Threads of Joy

In the cradle of the ancient hills,
Where silence breathes and spirit fills,
Tiruvannamalai, a flame in the dusk,
A sacred hymn, beyond earthly husk.

Granite giants touch the azure sky,
Veiled in whispers, secrets linger nigh,
Mighty Arunachala, your presence is profound,
In stillness, the heart of the world resounds.

Footprints of sages on timeless stone,
Echoes of seekers who walked alone,
With minds unshackled, they climbed your heights,
In pursuit of truth beyond the night.

Lanterns of faith flicker in the night,
Devotees gather, hearts burning bright,
Prayers unfurl like petals in bloom,
As the fragrant dawn dispels the gloom.

The winding paths, woven with grace,
Each step a prayer, each glance a trace,
Of love transcending the limits of time,
In the dance of existence, so pure, so sublime.

Cows wander freely, soft grass beneath,
While temple bells ring, weaving the wreath,
Of soulful offerings in the cool breeze,
As nature's orchestra plays with ease.

Oh, Tiruvannamalai, cradle of peace,
In your embrace, troubling thoughts cease,
For here, in your light, souls come to know,
The essence of being, the ebb and flow.

Let us gather our hopes, fears intertwined,
In the heart of your mountain, solace we find,
In the warmth of your hearth, love's tender sighs,
We lose our way, only to rise.

A pilgrimage, perhaps, of the heart and the mind,
In the glow of your aura, all beings aligned,
For in every sunrise that paints the sky blue,
There's a whisper of home, a promise anew.

12

Radiant Revelations: Unity in Glow

On the shimmering slope of the hill,
Where shadows twirl in luminous glow,
The embers glow with a scarlet shine,
Hints of comfort, a fresh promise divine.

The fire snaps and roars, fierce and free,
A core of nature, wild and stylishly,
Each spark recounts an ancient lore,
Of dreams set ablaze, and bravery at the core.

As evening falls, the sky dons a veil,
The atmosphere teems with tales to unveil,
The hill rises tall, a beacon so bright,
A refuge of peace, where souls unite.

In the cloak of night, the flames shine bright,
Within its heat, our souls unite,
We come together, cherished companions,
By the flickering light, our troubles vanish.

Thus, let us ascend the fiery rise,
In its glow, we'll hold no disguise,
For within the flame, we stand as a whole,
A celebration of life, until the light of day.

Elysian Echoes from Arunachala's Apex

Hark, what high peak doth pierce the blue skies?
'Tis Arunachala, famed in ancient lore,
Where Shiva's fiery form in stillness lies,
And pilgrims come, his grace to implore.

A granite brow, 'neath sun's bright golden ray,
They stand majestic, silent, and profound.
The verdant slopes where gentle breezes play,
With sacred whispers echoing all around.

The devotee, with a humble, contrite heart,
Doth tread the path that circles its base.
Each step a prayer, a casting off of smart,
Seeking the Lord in this most holy place.

The air is thick with incense, sweet and rare,
A fragrant offering to the Power divine.
And in the stillness, banished is all care,
As souls in reverence to this Mount incline.

Thus, let us gaze upon this wondrous sight,
This sacred hill, where peace doth ever dwell.
May Arunachala's grace, both pure and bright,
Within our hearts, a lasting story to tell.

Mindful Peaks: Echoes of Arunachala

Upon a hill, where shadows play,
Arunachala, bathed in a golden ray,
A revered peak, a mystical sight,
Where ancient souls ignite.

From lush green slopes to the heavens so high,
A mountain's essence, where mysteries lie,
With whispers soft and breezes free,
A timeless grace with eternal glee.

The sun ascends, its fiery kiss,
Upon the rocks, a golden bliss,
The air grows warm, the silence deep,
Where devotees pay their homage, heap.

A thousand hopes, a fervent plea,
To Arunachala, untamed and free,
For solace sought, and wisdom's light,
To guide the path in the darkest night.

The hill stands tall, a steadfast friend,
A holy space, where tranquillity transcends,
A timeless echo, soft and low,
Arunachala, where spirits flow.

With every dawn and every star,
The mountain's heart, forever far,
A luminous guide, a helping hand,
Mount Arunachala, across the land.

15

Tapestry of Triumph: Weaving Joy in Girivalam's Glow

In twilight's hush, where shadows dance and play,
Girivalam's mystic charm begins its sway.

With every step, a story unfolds like a tale,
Of devotion, love, and the heart that prevails.

The devotees walk, with feet bare and bright,
Their faith is a beacon, shining through the night.

Their eyes closed tight, their hearts full of cheer,
They chant the names of Lord Shiva, step by step.

The wind whispers secrets as they make their way,
Through the winding path, to the temple's sacred day.

The stars above twinkle like diamonds so fine,
Reflecting the beauty of this sacred shrine.

The trees stand tall, like sentinels of old,
Guarding the mysteries of stories yet untold.

The river flows, like a lifeline so true,
Quenching the thirst of souls anew.

The devotees bathe in its holy stream's flow,
Purifying themselves for the journey to know.

With each step forward, their spirit starts to rise,
As they surrender to the divine surprise.

Their footsteps echo, through the stillness of the night,
A symphony, of devotion, a wondrous sight.

The temple bells ring out with joyful sound,
As the devotees gather around the sacred ground.

Their prayers and hymns, a chorus of delight,
Filling the air with an otherworldly light.

The Girivalam path winds through hills so green,
A serpent's path, leads to the divine serene.

The devotees follow, with hearts full of glee,
Drinking in the beauty of nature's symmetry.

Their laughter echoes, through the valleys below,
As they dance and sing, with spirit aglow.

Their footsteps merge into one single stream,
A river of devotion, that knows no dream.

The Girivalam magic is a spell so strong,
That it weaves a tapestry, all day long.

It's a journey within, to the depths of the soul,
Where the divine resides, making us whole.

So, let us join hands in this sacred stride,
And walk the Girivalam path, side by side.

16

Echoes of Arrival: The Homeward Prayer

Upon a highland, bathed in the sun's embrace,
A mountain rises, a sacred, holy space.
Arunachala, a guiding light, bold and bright,
A timeless presence, illuminated by dawn's light.

From faraway lands, the pilgrims' footsteps tread,
Seeking solace, wisdom, and understanding bred.
Upon its heights, a silent prayer takes flight,
A gentle longing, bathed in sacred light.

The wind shares tales of ages long gone by,
Of ancient hymns that resonate to the sky.
The granite core, a bastion strong and deep,
Where secrets slumber, secrets yet to keep.

With every sunrise, painted hues unfold,
A tapestry of colours, stories told.
The shadows sway as twilight gently descends,
And Arunachala watches as the world enthrals.

A symphony of nature, soft and low,
The calm breeze, the rustling leaves that flow.
A sacred refuge, where peace and solace dwell,
Arunachala, a centre of the heavens' spell.

In every stone, a history untold,
A timeless presence, stories yet to be unfold.
An everlasting essence, stories waiting to be revealed.
Arunachala, a guiding force.

17

Between the Earthly Ties & Ethereal Skies: The Legacy of Ramana and His Mother

Azhagammal, a village wife,
Embraced the burdens of her life.

In Tiruchuli, 'midst temple bells,
A son was born, whose story tells.

Of silence deep and wisdom bright,
Venkataraman, bathed in inner light.

Her world was small, her duties clear,
To nurture him, to hold him dear.

She saw a child, so quick and keen,
With eyes that held a world unseen.

A playful boy, yet strangely still,
Obedient and of iron will.

His father died, a sudden blow,
Leaving her adrift in the depths of woe.

The family scattered, fortune waned,
Young Venkataraman remained,

Aloof, detached, in silent grace,
A distant look upon his face.

He moved to Madurai, his uncle's care,
But worldly things, he could not bear.

A sudden fear, a brush with death,
Awakened truths, beyond all breath.

The flame ignited, fierce and bold,
A story waiting to unfold.

He sought the Self with the burning quest,
Ignoring all, putting faith to the test.

A note he left, a simple plea,
"I go to seek my Father, He…"

Leaving behind the familiar shore,
To find the truth he yearned for.

He went to Arunachala's peak,
Where silent mountains softly speak.

And there he sat, in deep repose,
The ego stilled; the suffering slows.

Mouna, the silence, his only speech,
Beyond the grasp, beyond the reach.

Of worldly minds, that crave and cling,
To fleeting joys, that sorrow bring.

They called him mad; they saw him strange,
A boy withdrew, in life's exchange.

But in that madness, lay a key,
To liberation, wild and free.

His mother heard, the whispered tales,
Of sadhus strange, beyond the veils.

Of one who sat, in a silent trance,
Lost to the world, in mystic dance.

She yearned to see, her absent son,
To bring him back, to where he'd begun.

A mother's heart, knows no bounds,
It seeks its own, in hallowed grounds.

For years she lived, with hope and fear,
Imagining him, always near.

Meanwhile, on Arunachala's slope,
He taught in silence, giving hope.

Through piercing gaze, and gentle smile,
He led the seekers, mile by mile.

To turn within, to find the Self,
To shed the ego, like discarded pelf.

His body thinned, his hair grew long,
His voice was still, his spirit strong.

He lived on alms, a simple fare,
Beyond all want, beyond compare.

Then one day, Azhagammal came,
To find her son, and speak his name.

She saw him there, a silent sage,
A youth transformed, on life's grand stage.

Her heart cried out, in mingled pain,
And longing love, a sweet refrain.

"My son, my son," she softly wept,
"Why have you left, while others slept?"

He looked at her, with eyes of grace,
And in his gaze, she saw her face.

Reflected back, a mirrored soul,
Released from bondage, taking whole.

The truth that lay, within her breast,
A quiet calm, a peaceful rest.

She pleaded then, with mother's might,
To bring him back, to her light.

To leave this life, of solitude,
And share with her, the earthly good.

But he remained, in silent sway,
His purpose is clear, come what may.

He could not leave, his chosen path,
To quell the ego's aftermath.

He had to be, the guiding star,
To show the world, just who they are.

For years she stayed, around him near,
Her maternal love, dispelling fear.

He watched her age, with gentle care,
A silent witness to despair.

She sought release, from worldly ties,
To break the chains, before her eyes.

She learned from him, the subtle art,
Of stilling mind, and playing her part.

The Ashram grew, into a place of peace,
Where weary souls, found sweet release.

And Azhagammal, within its fold,
A story of transformation told.

She cooked and cleaned, she served the poor,
Her love a balm, forevermore.

She watched him teach, with silent might,
And slowly glimpsed his inner light.

The ego waned, the desires fled,
As peace descended, overhead.

She longed to know, the truth he held,
The secret whispered, truths compelled.

He saw her yearning, deep and true,
And guided her, to see anew.

To look within, to find the source,
Of all existence, and its force.

The 'Who am I?' a question posed,
To break the illusion, closely closed.

To trace the thought, back to its root,
And find the Self, the absolute.

She practiced well, with a steadfast mind,
Leaving the world, far behind.

Until at last, the day arrived,
When Azhagammal, nearly deprived.

Of mortal strength, began to fade,
Her earthly journey, was nearly paid.

She lay in pain, with laboured breath,
Approaching close, the gates of death.

But Ramana stayed, beside her bed,
His silent presence gently spread.

He placed his hand, on her chest,
And guided her, to a peaceful rest.

He helped her pierce, the final veil,
To find the Self, beyond the pale.

To merge with Brahman, pure and bright,
Released from darkness, into light.

Azhagammal, no longer bound,
In freedom vast, her spirit crowned.

Her body was buried, near the hall,
A temple was built, to honour all.

A mother's love transformed and pure,
A beacon bright, forever sure.

Sri Ramana, the silent sage,
Who turned a page, in history's age?

He showed the world, the path within,
To conquer death, and truly win.

A mother's blessing, ever near,
A guiding light to conquer fear.

So let us learn, from this divine,
And let our inner light truly shine.

18

Luminous Landscapes:
Celebrating Arunai's Essence

Where emerald hill meets sapphire skies so bright,
A whispered elegance, a luminous, ethereal light.
Arunai's touch, a gentle, flowing brook,
A whispered promise, a vibrant nook.

Through verdant valleys, where wildflowers delicately bloom,
His whisper echoes a celestial perfume.
A whispered secret, borne by the breeze,
Of ancient legends, rustling through the woods.

His ruby tones, a blazing, passionate art,
Reflecting sunsets, engraved upon the heart.
A symphony of hues, rich and profound,
Where nature's canvas secrets softly guards.

The mountain's shadow, a protective hand,
Upon his beauty, across the fertile land.
A timeless tapestry, woven thread by thread,
Arunai's splendour, is forever to be read.

From dawn's first blush to twilight's gentle sigh,
His grace unfolds beneath the watchful sky.
A shining gem, a treasure to behold,
Arunai's spirit, is forever to unfold.

19

Inhaling Grace & Exhaling Adventures: The Dance Beneath Eternal Skies

On the peak, where shadows dance,
A holy flame, burning at each glance.
Arunachala, towering and bright,
Where Shiva's essence fills the light.

A mystical vibe, gentle and profound,
Where ancient mysteries rest unbound.
The seeker's spirit finds true peace,
In Shiva's grace, forever will increase.

From distant lands, the faithful arrive,
With fiery hearts and souls to revive,
To discover the glow, the mighty force,
In Arunachala's treasured course.

The mantras resonate, soft and meek,
A melody of love, tender and sleek.
The hallowed stones, with ages, spun,
Stories shared by those who've run.

In every breath, a sacred plea,
To Shiva's grace, eternally free.
A timeless dance, beneath the sun,
Arunachala, forever won.

20

Tiruvannamalai: Chronicles of Light and Stone

On a majestic fire-kissed mountain,
Where ancient stones mutter a holy hand,
Tiruvannamalai, a beacon bright,
Shines forth in glory, bathed in early light.

From emerald slopes, where verdant valleys sleep,
To peaks that pierce the heavens, secrets keep,
A sacred space, where devotees convene,
To seek the solace and the grace within.

The air, perfumed with rich incense, sweet and deep,
Carries tales of hidden truth, they do keep,
Of Shiva's presence, ever strong and bold,
A narrative of ages, in stories told.

The Arunachala's form, a silhouette,
Against the sky, a sight to elevate,
An enduring presence, in a mystic hue,
A heart of sincere devotion, ever true.

Through winding routes, where pilgrims tread,
With faith as a compass, and hope as food,
They seek solace and peace within,
In Tiruvannamalai, where spirits spin.

Come and travel to this sacred place,
Where ancient wisdom finds its rightful space,
Tiruvannamalai, a timeless grace,
A ray of hope, in time and space.

21

Whispers of Wonderment: Revelling in Arunaigiri's Embrace

Upon Arunagiri's peak, where shadows softly creep,
A mystical power, a sacred sleep.
The dawn awakes, a golden hue,
On timeworn stones, a vision true.

From the depths of thought, a fervent plea,
For grace divine, eternal.
The saint's heart yearns, with a whispered prayer,
To Arunachala, banish care.

The mountain's brow, a radiant sight,
Illuminates the endless night.
With every beat, a rhythmic sound,
A holy ground, forever bound.

In Arunagiri's hallowed space,
A timeless grace, a sacred trace.
Where earthly troubles fade away,
And souls find comfort, come what may.

Climb the slopes with reverent tread,
And seek the peace that's overhead.
Within Arunagiri's sacred sphere,
A love profound dispels all fear.

22

Windswept Whispers: An Ode to Ancient Heights

The sun-kissed peaks, in golden light arrayed,
Reflect the heavens, softly, unafraid.
A tapestry of trees, in emerald green,
Where mysteries slumber, 'neath the whispering sheen.

The cool, crisp air, a balm upon the soul,
As ancient stories, softly start to roll.
Of legends, whispered, on the mountain's breast,
Of dancing spirits, put to gentle test.

From craggy heights, a panoramic view,
Of valleys slumbering, bathed in morning dew.
The distant villages, in clusters small,
A tapestry of life that stands so tall.

The mountain's heart, a symphony of sound,
Of rushing waters, echoes all around.
A vibrant pulse that beats with life's grace,
A sacred space, in time and time's embrace.

Come, dear traveller, to this hallowed ground,
Where peace resides and splendours of nature are found.
On Sonachala's slopes, let worries cease,
And find your solace, find your inner peace.

23

Echoes of Shiva: A Nature's Overture

Upon the peaks, where heavens meet the ground,
A mountain stands, a sacred, holy mount.
The mountain of Shiva, with majesty profound,
A fortress strong, with legends unbound.

Of emerald hues and granite, stark and grey,
It pierces the clouds, a titan on display.
With swirling mists that dance in sunlit ray.
A mystic aura fills the mountain's sway.

Since ancient times, its stories whispered low,
Of gods and demons, in a battle's flow.
Where sacred rivers, from its summit, flow,
And sacred chants, their echoes softly glow.

Shiva's grace, a symbol bold and bright,
A pillar piercing in the endless light.
With carvings deep, of figures fierce and grand,
A tapestry of tales across the land.

The mountain's heart, a furnace, fiery red,
Where secrets slumber, mysteries spread.
With temples carved in stone, so strong and true,
A sacred haven, where devotees accrue.

The wind howls, a mournful, eerie sound,
Across the slopes where echoes are unbound.
A symphony of nature, all around,
The mountain of Shiva, revered and crowned.

24

In the Embrace of Silence: Finding Light in Shadows

A mountain of quietude, stark and grand,
Where echoes rest, a whispered band.
No rushing stream, no windswept sigh,
Just granite peaks beneath the sky,
Of muted hue, a sombre grace,
A timeless stillness in this place.

The shadowy slopes, a velvet drape,
Conceal the secrets of the shape,
Of ancient stories, entombed deep,
Where whispers fade and secrets sleep.
No human voice, no bird's soft trill,
Just silent stones and mountain chill.

A solitude profound and vast,
Where thoughts are lost and memories cast,
Into the void, a fading gleam,
A silent vigil, a solemn dream.
The mountain holds its breath, serene,
A monument to what has been.

A timeless peace, a whispered prayer,
That echoes softly, year after year.
The mountain's heart, a hidden core,
Of silence deep, forevermore.
A sanctuary, vast and grand,
The mountain of silence, in the land.

25

The Sanctuary Within: A Haven for Hope's Whisper

A mountain of the self, so vast and deep,
Where secrets slumber, secrets we keep.
With jagged peaks of pride and valleys low,
Where shadows dance and whispers flow.

Its pinnacle, capped with dreams both grand and bold,
Where hopes reside, in stories yet untold.
Its base, a chasm, dark and full of fears,
Where doubts and worries shed their silent tears.

The slopes ascend, with trials hard and steep,
Where doubts and fears, like frigid winds, sweep.
Yet strength and courage, hidden deep within,
Can climb the heights and conquer every sin.

The mountain's heart, a furnace, burning bright,
With passions intense and guiding inner light.
A tapestry of thoughts, both dark and fair,
Interwoven with strands of joy and silent prayer.

On its slopes, we find our truest self,
A journey inward, a profound, deep self.
Where truth dwells, in quiet contemplation's grace,
A mountain's form, within a hidden space.

Climb this peak, this mountain of the soul,
And find the strength to make your spirit whole.
Embrace the shadows allow the light to take hold,
And in that journey, stories yet unfold.

Veiled Reflections: The Puzzle of Whom I Might Be?

A whisper faint, a fleeting thought,
A mosaic of stories wrought.
From childhood dreams to whispered fears,
A million selves, dissolving tears.

I pursue the sun, a fleeting gleam,
A shadowed form, a waking dream.
I build and break, I rise and fall,
A frail soul, answering a call.

Who am I? A query deep,
A mystery that secrets keep.
A canvas vast, with bright colours
Bathed in moonlight, filled with stars

I yearn for love, a kind hand,
To understand this shifting stand.
A restless heart, a wandering mind,
A soul entwined, forever kind.

I paint the world with hues of grace,
A fleeting moment, time and space.
A symphony of joy and pain,
A human heart, in endless reign.

Who am I? A question grand,
A whispered echo through the land.
A masterpiece, in time's embrace,
A transient soul, in time and space.

27

Mindful Wandering: Discovering Sri Ramana's Light

1. In deep silence, the heart learns to see,
   The self is not apart; it's meant to be.

2. Beyond all thoughts, where the mind falls still,
   The ego fades, and the soul finds its fill.

3. Ask who am I, let the question unfold,
   In seeking the truth, let your spirit be bold.

4. Dispel the shadows that cloud your pure sight,
   Within lies the answer, your essence shines bright.

5. The body is fleeting, like clouds in the sky,
   But the heart holds the timeless—let the worldly pass by.

6. In turning within, find the light of the soul,
   The universe whispers, "You are already whole."

7. Each breath is a passage, a step toward the known,
   In the stillness of being, you're never alone.

8. The seeker finds riches in silence and grace,
   Touch the depths of your being, and know your true face.

9. Let go of the seeker; let go of the sought,
   In the quiet of presence, what matters is caught.

10. The river of thought may rush and may roar,
    But still lies the ocean—unbounded, secure.

11. Ramana's wisdom—direct yet profound,
    Awakening echoes in the silence around.

12. To grasp is a veil; in surrender, you bloom,
    The Self is the answer - embrace the inner room.

13. In the mirror of stillness, your essence reflects,
    Forget all distractions, embrace the pretext.

14. As waves are to the oceans, the self is to all,
    Dive deep into awareness; you'll rise from the fall.

15. Recognize the essence, let the illusion fade,
    You are not the forms; the spirit won't trade.

16. In the vastness of being, find your rightful place,
    Each moment is a gateway to an unending embrace.

17. Through inquiry's lens, perception transforms,
    In the light of clarity, the heart gently warms.

18. Beyond the struggle, beyond all the strife,
    The Self is the stillness, the breath of true life.

19. The star of your being, forever it shines,
    In recognizing the whole, the separation unwinds.

20. The teachings of Ramana echo like a song,
    In the dance of existence, find where you belong.

21. So journey within, dear seeker, be brave,
    The Self is the whisper, the infinite wave.

28

Inward Bound: Still Waters Run Deep

In the sacred hold of Arunachala's grace,
A selfless spirit discovered a tranquil space.
Sri Ramana Maharshi, profound and bright,
Where quiet wisdom is hidden from the sight.

With gentle poise, a beacon of hope,
Eliminating darkness, helping hearts cope.
By engaging curious minds, he forged a path.
To the essence of truth and the light that lasts.

The true essence of the Self, bright and clear,
A radiant beacon, pure and near.
With gentle words, he shared his guide,
The way to tranquillity, the inner tide.

He sought to break free from worldly strife,
In the Self's embrace, discovered life.
An ageless sage, with love so deep,
His lessons resonate; securely keep.

Through the art of quiet reflection,
He revealed the heart, a heartfelt connection.
A brilliant mind, with insight vast,
The glow of his wisdom forever lasts.

Let us endeavour, with spirits free,
To uncover that lasting tranquillity.
For within the grace of Sri Ramana,
We uncover our Self through time's panorama.

SRI RAMANASRAMAM

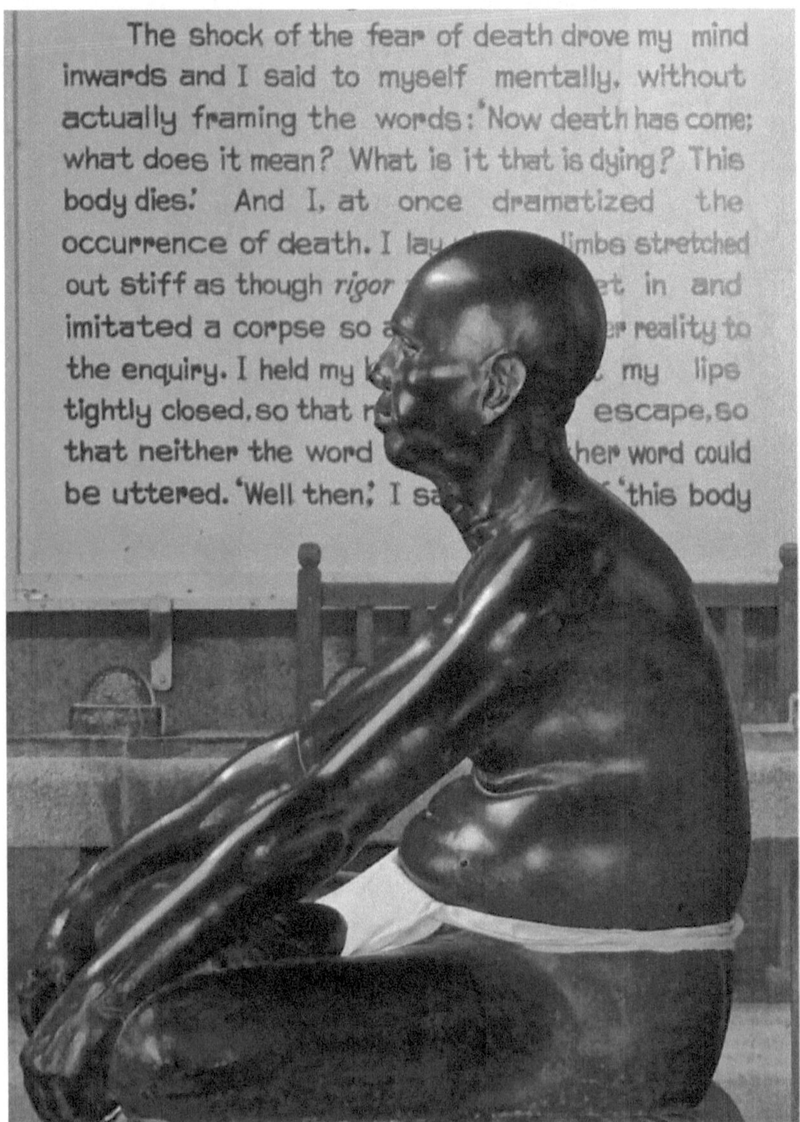
The shock of the fear of death drove my mind
inwards and I said to myself mentally, without
actually framing the words: 'Now death has come;
what does it mean? What is it that is dying? This
body dies.' And I, at once dramatized the
occurrence of death. I lay limbs stretched
out stiff as though rigor set in and
imitated a corpse so reality to
the enquiry. I held my my lips
tightly closed, so that escape, so
that neither the word her word could
be uttered. 'Well then,' I s 'this body

29

Embers of Enlightenment:
Arunachala's Flame-Fuelled Might

Arunachala, sacred hill of fire,
A beacon bright, one's heart's desire,
In the early light, you gently rise,
Veiled in mist beneath the skies.

Your rugged slopes, an enduring tale,
Whispers of saints through every vale,
The winds carry prayers, soft and low,
Where seekers tread, their spirits glow.

In twilight's embrace, you don your crown,
With a hint of gold, a rich, burnished brown,
The sun bids farewell, painting the night,
While stars awaken, twinkling bright.

O Hill of flame, with hallowed ground,
Where stillness speaks, and calm is found,
The ancient stones, with wisdom call,
In your presence, all worries fall.

From dawn to dusk, you remain so grand,
A watchful sentinel, above them all,
The seekers' journey, from far and near,
To uncover the truth, with hearts sincere.

The whispers of the temple chimes,
Echo tales that the spirit rhymes,
A sanctuary of love, a timeless place,
In your shadows, we discover your grace.

The rivers twirl, their waters bright,
Mirroring the beauty that brings delight,
The holy ash, the flames aglow,
In your warmth, we shed the woe.

Oh, Arunachala, your teachings prevail,
The heart of affection, the power to prevail,
In every dusk, in every dawn's start,
You are the enlightenment that never departs.

Call of the Unseen: A Symphony of the Self

From silent depths, a mountain beckons,
Arunachala, where the shadow falls.
A beacon bright, a fire's core,
That pulls the seeker to its shore.

No outward form can truly bind,
The grace that permeates the mind.
A golden hue at breaking dawn,
Where worldly worries fade and are gone.

The ancient stones, a silent sage,
Unfolding wisdom, page by page.
In still devotion, hearts take flight,
Towards the source of the purest light.

A presence vast, a silent might,
That turns the darkness into light.
Arunachala, a sacred name,
To find oneself and be the same.

Beyond the peak, beyond the stone,
A truth uncovered, widely known.
The self-revealed, in silent grace,
Within this holy, hallowed place.

Tiruvannamalai's Triumph: Where Heart's Ignite

At Arunachala's ancient, sacred peak,
Where Shiva's presence speaks, though lips are weak,
A beacon waits, a promise held in the flame,
Tiruvannamalai Deepam, whispered name.

For days, the preparations rise and swell,
Devotees gather stories they will tell,
Of grace bestowed, of burdens cast aside,
Beneath this mountain, where all truths reside.

The copper cauldron, filled with ghee so bright,
A thousand camphor flames ignite the night,
A crackling roar, a burst of golden grace,
Illuminating every timeworn face.

The signal given, from the sacred core,
The Deepam blazes, wanting nothing more,
Then to reflect the spirit, pure and true,
That dwells within Arunachala and you.

It burns for days, a steadfast, shining guide,
Across the valleys, where lost souls reside,
A gentle whisper, "Turn and look above,
Find solace there, in Arunachala's love."

Let us gaze upon this holy fire,
And let our hearts be lifted ever higher,
Toward the truth, the peace, the radiant light,
Of Tiruvannamalai, burning ever bright.

32

Echoes of Eternity: Ramana's Radiant Pathway

Mount Arunachala stands,
A beacon in these shifting sands.
Beneath its gaze, a soul took root,
Ramana, bearing silent fruit.

No worldly chase, no burning need,
Just stillness, planting wisdom's seed.
"Who am I?" is the constant quest,
A turning inward to find true rest.

He spoke with silence, eyes so deep,
Where restless thoughts would fall asleep.
No doctrines preached, no rigid creed,
Just simply pointing to the need.

To find the source, the 'I' within,
Where peace resides, untouched by sin.
The ego's clamour gently ceases,
And merge with the Source; find inner peace.

He lived the truth, a living flame,
A testament to God's name.
Ramana's grace, a gentle hand,
To guide lost souls to the Promised Land.

Look within, and ask yourself,
Beyond the stories on the shelf.
The answer lies not far away,
In silence deep, where truths hold sway.

33

No Rituals Required:
Awakening Through Awareness

A mountain's gaze, a silent grace,
Sri Ramana, in timeless space.
No sermon loud, no frantic plea,
Just stillness deep, for all to see.

The gaze that pierced beyond the shell,
To the Atman, where true truths dwell.
"Who am I?" the question keen,
To unravel the ego, unseen.

Arunachala, the fire hill,
A magnet drawing, at His will.
Around its slopes, in humble shade,
The seekers gather, unafraid.

He spoke in silence, understood,
A mirror held, for inner good.
No grand rituals, no sacred rites,
But self-inquiry, burning bright.

To find the source, the 'I' within,
Where peace resides, and all begins.
Sri Ramana, a beacon's gleam,
Awakening us from a dream.

Breathe it in, the quiet air,
And find the Self, beyond compare.
A mountain's strength, a loving hand,
Sri Ramana, in this sacred land.

34

Whisper from Heights: A Journey to Self, Amidst Slopes

Verdant crown of leafy green,
But granite grey, a timeless scene.
A beacon raised against the sky,
Where ancient wisdom starts to fly.

The sun descends, a molten kiss,
Igniting peaks with fervent bliss.
A blush of rose, a crimson stain,
Washing away the worldly pain.

Devotees walk, a mindful tread,
Circumnavigating, prayers are said.
Each step is a cleansing, slow, and deep,
A promise whispered, secrets kept.

Arunachala, a fire bright,
Consuming darkness, bringing light.
A mountain sleeps, yet ever awake,
A burning heart, for goodness' sake.

Climb its slopes, or walk below,
Feel the power, the gentle flow.
Let Arunachala's spirit bind,
And leave the earthly world behind.

35

Who Am I?: Thoughts Beneath the Ramana Lingam's Light

From Arunachala's heart, a silent grace,
Ramana Lingam, in a sacred space.
No bustling words, no outward show,
Just Being's light, a gentle glow.

His eyes, a depth where silence sleeps,
A wisdom born from mountain keeps.
No creed he preached, no dogma's chain,
Just "Who am I?" again and again.

He drew the seekers to his side.
Where ego's waves could gently glide?
Into the stillness, vast and deep,
Where truth resides and secrets slip.

A lingam formed, a silent guide,
To turn within, where selves reside.
Ramana's grace, a steady beam,
Awakening from a waking dream.

Seek the source, the "I" within,
Let the questioning begin, and let it spin.
A thread of truth, to lead your home,
Where peace and love forever roam.

Ramana Lingam, a silent call,
To find one's self, and be it all.
The mountain stands, a timeless sign,
Of the eternal and the divine.

36

Flames Enduring Light: Love Beyond Death's Doorway

In the shadow of the mountain high,
Where whispers of the silence sigh,
There stands a spirit, pure and bright,
Arunachala, a guiding light.

With every dawn that graces the land,
The sage arose with a gentle hand,
A seeker lost in the quest for the soul,
In the heart of the hills, he found his whole.

Ramana spoke of the inner way,
To look within, to find the sway,
In every thought, in every breath,
He showed the path that conquers death.

Devotees gather, with hearts sincere,
Offering prayers, their doubts clear,
With eyes lifted to the peak,
In stillness divine, the truth they seek.

The echoes of silence, the song of the wise,
In Arunachala's grasp, the spirit lies,
A flame of wisdom, forever it glows,
In the hearts of the seekers, the love ever grows.

Mindscapes of Maharshi: Mapping the Inner Cosmos

In the hallowed land of Tiruvannamalai,
Where ancient mountains cast their shade,
Resided Ramana, a deep spirit,
His insight shining, ever unafraid.

A young seeker aimed to uncover the truth,
Within the tangled paths of existence,
He turned his back on worldly youth.
To dedicate his days to quiet reverence.

He ascended the heights of Arunachala.
And there he remained, under the sun's glow,
His expression was tranquil, with a magnificent aura.
His internal calm was already aglow.

The years rolled on, the seasons turned,
Devotees came from far and near,
His simple words, their spirits burned,
To shed their doubts and conquer fear.

No grand pronouncements did he make.
No doctrines preached, or scriptures read,
He showed the way, for goodness's sake,
To find the self within the head.

With gentle eyes and loving grace,
He taught the path to liberation.
A smiling face, in time and space,
A beacon of pure contemplation.

He melted hearts; he calmed all strife.
A silent sage, a guiding light,
He lived a life beyond all life,
And showed the way to inner sight.

So, pilgrims come, and still they pray,
To Arunachala's holy peak,
Remembering Ramana's gentle way,
The peace he found was so pure and meek.

Fragments of Truth: Shattered Mirrors in Silent Reflections

From the hallowed soil of Tiruvannamalai,
A sage of silence, both revered and wise.
Young Ramana, a spirit ablaze,
Pursued the truth with an unwavering gaze.

He renounced the transient world around,
Embracing the sacred light of Arunachala's ground.
Living simply, with a humble view,
He immersed himself in the self as days flew.

Inquiries arose from distant and near,
In search of wisdom, radiant and clear.
With soft-spoken words or a tranquil glance,
He directed seekers to their inner expanse.

No doctrines imposed, nor dogmas to bind,
Just a journey of self-inquiry, day by day defined.
He guided hearts to discover their light,
Leaving behind all concepts and taking flight.

Devotees gathered, a devoted crowd,
Eager to absorb his teachings, profound and loud.
From various lands, they ventured to see,
The strength is found in his simplicity.

His silence conveyed a mystical grace,
Awakening slumbering hearts in their place.
Words were unnecessary; the truth shone bright,
In the stillness, dispelling all fright.

He led a life of tranquillity and depth.
His wisdom is a treasure, secret adept.
Arunachala remained his steadfast guide.
A timeless essence, forever inside.

Though he has departed, his spirit endures.
A radiant beacon through the years, it ensures.
The Guru's grace, a gentle embrace,
Leads seekers onward, across every space.

Thus, let us heed the path of Ramana.
To uncover the Self and illuminate the dawn.
In stillness, the answers await our quest.
Beneath the boundless and infinite crest.

39

The Stillness Within: Arunachala's Whispering Wisdom for Busy Minds

In the heart of the land where the sun gently rises,
Lies a mountain bold, where truth never disguises.
A sentinel of peace, with its peaks touching time,
A witness to the ages and the rhythm of rhyme.

Its slopes whisper tales of sages and seers.
Of meditative minds and the dissolving of fears.
In the stillness of dusk, where shadows softly play,
The mountain breathes wisdom at the end of the day.

Clouds float by, like dreams on a gentle breeze.
As nature sings a lullaby amidst the swaying trees.
Birds carry notes of an ancient, sacred song,
While the mountain stands steadfast, timeless, and strong.

The sun dips low, painting the skies with hues of gold,
As the night wraps the mountain in its comforting fold.
Stars emerge like diamonds on the velvet sky.
Guardians of secrets that never say goodbye.

Here, under the watchful gaze of the moon's soft glow,
Lies the heart of the earth, where pure waters flow.
A sacred bond between the sky and the earth,
A place of rebirth, where souls find their worth.

In the silence of night, where the heartbeats of time pause,
The mountain whispers truths, a sacred, eternal cause.
To those who seek with open hearts, it shows the way.
A guiding light till the break of day.

As dawn paints the horizon with colours anew,
The mountain stands witness, a timeless view.
A beacon of hope, amidst the eternal cha-cha,
In the land where the spirit finds peace—Arunachala.

40

Celestial Calm: Where Shadows Fade into Radiance

In a realm where seekers gather, hearts ignited,
To uncover truths, a name softly recited,
The master's essence, profound and serene,
In tranquil reflection, hidden wisdom is gleaned.

The venerable walls, steeped in ancient lore,
Reveal the journey of wisdom's core,
Attracting seekers from distant lands,
In pursuit of solace, to heal their hands.

The atmosphere resonates with sacred power.
A gentle vibration, a guiding tower,
In stillness, the solutions reside,
Beneath the celestial expanse, far and wide.

The hallowed ash, a radiant sign,
Of truth's warm embrace, a joy divine,
A haven of peace, serene and blessed,
Where tranquillity reigns and souls find rest.

Freed from worldly burdens, the mind takes flight,
In stillness, the spirit finds delight,
Sri Ramanasramam, a true refuge,
Where inner harmony continually ensues.

41

The Madurai Awakening: Transforming the Fear of Death

I.

Young Venkataraman, in slumber deep,
A sudden fear, the breath ceased to keep.
Yet in that stillness, a radiant light,
Revealed the Self, serene and ever bright.

II.

The frail body lay still and cold, they thought.
But within bloomed a wisdom dearly bought.
The 'I' that binds, dissolved in grace,
Leaving pure Being in its sacred space.

III.

From the mortal coil, the spirit took its flight,
Not into darkness, but into endless light.
The fear of death, a phantom, took its leave,
As the true Self, he came to perceive.

IV.

The bustling city, Madurai's vibrant hum,
Faded as inner silence had become.
His constant guide, his solace, and his stay,
Transformed forever from that fateful day.

V.

No outward journey, no arduous quest,
But inward turning, he put his soul at rest.
The blissful state, a natural unfold,
A story whispered, centuries old.

42

Whispers of the Wild:
Sri Ramana's Compassion

At Arunachala's feet, a sage serene,
Sri Ramana, where love was ever seen.

Not just for humans did his wisdom flow,
But for all creatures, both high and low.

A cow named Lakshmi held a sacred place,
Within his heart, a gentle, warm embrace.

Monkeys would gather, curious and bold,
Their stories told, in ways untold.

Squirrels would scamper, unafraid and free,
Beneath the gaze of his tranquillity.

Dogs found refuge, loyal and so true,
Knowing kindness in all he'd do.

He'd share his food with creatures near,
Dispelling hunger, calming every fear.

No separation did his vision hold,
All beings are sacred stories to unfold.

He saw the Atman, shining bright and clear.
In every creature, casting out all fear.

A wounded bird, he nursed with loving care,
Demonstrating compassion, beyond compare.

The silent language, he so understood,
Of every creature, in the field and wood.

He taught us oneness, a truth profound,
Where love and kindness endlessly abound.

So let us learn, from Ramana's gentle way,
To treat all beings with respect each day.

43

Sri Ramanasramam: Serenity in the Shadows of Arunachala

In Tiruvannamalai's sacred land,
Where Arunachala's Mountain stands,
A haven for seekers, pure and bright,
Sri Ramanasramam shines with a soothing light.

Its gates, a threshold to the soul,
Invite the weary to make whole,
Their hearts, aflame with love's desire,
To find the Self, they owe true fire.

The samadhi hall, a peaceful nest,
Enshrines the sage, forever at rest,
His presence still, a guiding ray,
Illuminates the seeker's way.

The old hall, where devotees would meet,
And listen to his words so sweet,
Now echoes with memories past,
Of laughter, tears, and moments that last.

The dining hall, where meals are shared,
A time for the community to be spared,
Simple food, yet love abounds,
Nourishing body, heart, and mind.

The gardens bloom, vibrant and fair,
A reflection of the peace that's there,
Trees sway gently, leaves rustle free,
As nature's beauty whispers secrets to thee.

At dusk, the temple's bell tolls deep,
Calling all to meditation's keep,
The stars appear, like diamonds bright,
As seekers sit, immersed in the tranquillity of the night.

At Sri Ramanasramam, time stands still.
As hearts and minds converge to fulfil,
The longing for the ultimate goal,
Self-realization, the eternal role.

44

Sri Ramanasramam: Oasis of Truth Beneath the Ancient Peak

In the heart of silence, where the mountains rise,
Beneath the watchful gaze of the endless skies,
Lies a sanctuary woven in shadows and light,
The Ashram of Ramana, a beacon so bright.

Here, the air is thick with the fragrance of prayer.
As seekers arrive with burdens to share.
With hearts full of questions, like birds in a cage,
They come to unravel the threads of their age.

The stillness enchants, like a soft summer breeze,
Each mantra and murmur bring a gentle unease.
In the temple of wisdom, where time seems to stall,
The whispers of sages invite one and all.

Oh, Ramana's sweet presence, a fire in the night,
With eyes of quiet knowing, reflecting the light.
He beckons us inward, where ego must cease,
In the depths of our being, we may find our release.

The sun dips low, painting the rocks with gold,
As stories of seekers throughout the ages unfold.
From the depths of the asana, the soul takes its flight,
Tracing the contours of unending delight.

In the gardens of bliss, where the sacred drum beats,
Each heartbeat is a prayer, in the world of retreats.
From the lessons of love to the dance of despair,
The Ashram embraces a cradle of care.

Linger we must, in this hallowed embrace,
As time dissolves softly in the stillness of grace.
For in Ramana's wisdom, the truth shall be found.
In the depth of our silence, in the oneness around.

45

Beneath the Banyan's Shade:
A Celebration of Stillness

Under Arunagiri's banyan shade so grand,
Four sages sit in contemplation's stand,
Their eyes closed tight, their souls take flight,
As wisdom whispers secrets through the night.

Their robes are worn, their beards long and grey,
Their hearts filled with the knowledge of the day,
They've walked the earth, they've seen it all,
And in their silence, truth stands bold and tall.

With eyes that see beyond time and space,
The four sages ponder life's great pace,
Their minds afire with questions yet untold,
Their spirits soaring like the eagle bold.

Agni, Vayu, Jala, and Akasha too,
The elements they represent, pure and true,
Their balance and harmony, the key to the land,
Arunagiri's sages understand, hand in hand.

In this sacred place, where ancient trees preside,
The four sages meditate, side by side,
Their wisdom flows like a river wide,
Guiding seekers on their inner tide.

As sunbeams filter through the leafy branches above,
The sages smile, their hearts full of love,
For they know the mysteries of the universe deep,
And share their insights, in silence they keep.

Eyes that Illuminate: The Beacon Beneath Arunachala's Skies

From Arunachala's foot, a beacon brightly shone,
Sri Ramana, the sage, his wisdom deeply sown.
A silent master, eyes that pierced the soul,
Unravelling the ego, making spirits whole.
In Tiruvannamalai, his presence did reside,
A magnet for the seekers, truths have nowhere to hide.
Venkatraman, the boy, surrendered to the fire.
Of self-inquiry, fuelling his desire.

His teachings echoed, "Who am I?" the guiding light,
A path of self-discovery, banishing the night.
No rituals were prescribed, and no scriptures were held as law.
Just introspection deep, transcending every flaw.
He sat in stillness, a mountain strong and tall,
Absorbing sorrows, answering every call.
His devotees gathered, drawn by grace untold,
Listening to silence is more precious than pure gold.

Lakshmi the cow, the squirrels, and the stray dogs, too,
Found solace in his presence, feeling loved and true.
Ganapati Muni, a scholar of renown,
Found Ramana's wisdom, wearing the ego's crown.

He whispered "Bhagavan," a title from the heart,
A humble recognition, setting him apart.
His body withered, yet his spirit soared above,
Eternal, boundless, embracing with its love.

The cancer claimed his form, the physical facade,
But Ramana's Self remained, forever vowed.
He demonstrated, truly, what it means to be free.
Beyond the body's limits, eternally.
So, let us bow in reverence to this master kind,
Who opened up the gateway for peace to find?
Sri Ramana Maharshi, our Guru, true and bright,
Guiding us to freedom, bathed in Self's pure light.

47

In Stillness: The Divine Lesson Emerges

In the shade of a banyan, ancient, vast,
A silent teacher, wisdom cast.
Sri Dakshina Moorthy, form divine,
Where stillness speaks, and truths align.

His youthful face, a paradox,
Eternity within Him locks.
No words he utters, lips remain,
A silent lesson, ease from pain.

The aged rishis gathered near,
Drink nectar where all doubts disappear.
Guru Upadesa whispered deep,
Knowledge is sown while senses sleep.

Through mudras, eloquent and bright,
He guides the seekers towards the light.
Jnana Mudra, circle formed,
The Atman, Brahman, is now transformed.

The universe within the Self,
Forgotten truths upon the shelf,
Awakened by His silent grace,
A smile that time cannot erase.

No scriptures read, no rituals done,
But understanding is brightly spun.
From heart to heart, the wisdom flows,
The seed of liberation grows.

Dakshina Moorthy, silent guide,
Where ego melts on ignorance's tide.
A beacon burning ever clear,
Dispelling darkness, calming fear.

Seek the silence, look within,
And find the Guru deep within.
For Upadesa, true and bold,
A story in His silence told.

48

Mountain Melodies: The Heartbeat of Earth's Quietude

Beneath the vast sky where eagles dare to soar,
Stands a sentinel of silence, rich in ancient lore.
Arunagiri, a beacon bright, in twilight's soft embrace,
A mountain celebrated by poets' hearts, a sacred space.

Your slopes are draped in emerald dreams, where gentle breezes
    sigh,
And every stone, a tale to tell, as time flows quietly by.
The dawn adorns your wreathed face with shades of rose and
    gold.
While shadows dance in twilight's grace, with stories yet untold.

Each step upon your rugged path brings echoes from the past,
Of brave seekers who climbed your heights, their spirits held
    steadfast.
In twilight's arms, they found their voice, their aches, their joys,
    their fears,
Transforming silence into songs that mingle with mountain tears.

The temple bells ring out above, their chimes a tender prayer,
For every heart that seeks your peace, for every soul laid bare.
In moments hushed, as day departs, the stars begin to weave,
A tapestry of all that's lost, of all that we believe.

Oh, Arunagiri, wise cradle, you keep our dreams aglow,
The yearning hearts, the wandering souls, forever in your flow.
In every leaf, in every stone, in every breath we take,
Your presence lingers, a melody, in each dawn we awake.

Here we stand, with minds unchained, as poetry takes flight,
In Arunagiri's gentle arms, we find our world of light.
Through whispered words and heartfelt sighs, let songs of love
    resound,
For in your embrace, dear bold mountain, a deeper truth is found.

49

Whisper from Heights: A Journey to Self, Amidst Slopes

In twilight's hush, where shadows play,
Amidst the whispers of a fading day,
A mystic mountain stands, serene and tall,
Sacred Sonachalam, hear its call.

A place of ancient wisdom, born of the earth,
Where echoes of the past give gentle birth,
To whispers of the gods and secrets untold,
In Sonachalam's heart, the mysteries unfold.

The wind that whispers through its leafy trees,
Carries the prayers of countless knees,
That have bowed down in reverence and awe,
To the sacred energies that in silence draw.

The sun rises, painting the sky,
With hues of crimson, gold, and morning's sigh,
Awakens the soul to the beauty and might,
Of Sonachalam's splendour, a wondrous sight.

In this sacred land, where myth and magic blend,
The boundaries of time and space transcend,
The seeker's heart, with wonder and peace,
Finds solace in the stillness, the world's wild release.

Oh, Sonachalam, your beauty we adore,
A haven for the soul, forever in store,
A place of pilgrimage, for heart and mind,
Where the divine and human, in harmony, entwine.

May the essence of your sacred spirit stay,
With those who seek and find their way,
To the depths of their own heart, where love resides,
And in Sonachalam's silence, their soul abides.

From Shadows to Sunlight: Arunachala's Gentle Grace

In ancient days of yore, beneath the skies,
Tiruvannamalai stood, a hill so grand.
Its sacred peaks where eternal light lies,
A beacon for seekers in every land.

The hill, a symbol of divine embrace,
Whispers of wisdom carried through the breeze.
With each ascent, we find our inner grace,
And burdens lift as hearts are set at ease.

From dawn till dusk, its shadows cast their spell,
Guiding pilgrims on paths both steep and vast.
In silence there, the soul begins to dwell,
And all life's doubts dissolve away at last.

Beneath its gaze, the fire within ignites,
A spark of truth that burns through the darkest night.
The journey up unveils celestial heights,
Where man and mountain merge in the sacred rite.

By moonlit nights or sun-drenched days anew,
Tiruvannamalai stands tall and wise.
A timeless sentinel with a steadfast view,
Granting seekers peace under open skies.

51

Her Sacred Heartbeat:
Tales of Mother Unnamulai

In southern lands, where sunbeams gleam,
A temple stood, a sacred dream.
Unnamulai Amman, the goddess bright,
Her presence shone, a holy light.

A humble farmer, worn and old,
His fields lay barren, stories told,
Of failing crops and dwindling store,
His heart was heavy, evermore.

His wife, so frail, with eyes so dim,
Cried silent tears, her spirit grim.
Their children watched with a hungry gaze,
Through sun-scorched days and starless haze.

He journeyed then, with weary feet,
To seek the goddess, humbly greet.
Her sacred shrine implores her grace,
To save his family from this hard phase.

He knelt and prayed, with fervent plea,
"Oh, Mother Unnamulai, hear me, see me!
My life is spent, my hope is low,
My family suffers; grant them flow.

The goddess heard his heartfelt cry,
A gentle breeze swept through the sky.
A golden light, a mystic ray,
Illumined him, that very day.

A vision then, before he spread,
A field of gold, where harvests were bred,
Abundant grain, a joyful sight,
Dispelling shadows, dark as night.

He woke refreshed; his spirit soared.
The goddess' message, he implored,
To carry forth, to spread the word,
Of her compassion, gently heard.

He hurried home, his footsteps light,
With hope renewed and shining bright.
He reached his fields with a trembling hand,
And found the change across the land.

The withered stalks had sprung anew,
With emerald leaves and glistening dew.
The golden grain, in heavy ears,
Erased his fears and calmed all his tears.

His wife embraced him, overjoyed.
Their children laughed, no longer void,
Of food and comfort, warmth and cheer,
Mother Unnamulai's grace banished all fear.

The village folk, gathered near,
To hear the story, far and clear.
Of farmer's faith and goddess' might,
That banished darkness brought the light.

And so, they sang, in joyful praise,
Of Mother Unnamulai, through all their days.
A sacred legend passed along,
In grateful hearts, a grateful song.

The temple bells, their voices chime,
A testament to passing time,
Of faith and hope, and goddess' grace,
That blessed the land, time, and space.

And to this day, the story rings,
Of Mother Unnamulai's healing wings,
A symbol bright, forever true,
Of hope and faith, for me and you.

52

Chants of Chaos: The Battle Hymns of Bhairava's Seven

The Fierce Guardian
With eyes that burn like cosmic fire,
And fangs that gleam with righteous ire,
He stands as the guardian, strong and bold.
Protecting devotees, young and old.

The Lord of Time
Beyond the grasp of transient moments,
He reigns where time itself disappears.
Oh, Bhairava, the endless flow,
Where all beginnings and all endings go.

The Dispeller of Fear
In blackest nights, when shadows creep,
And anxious thoughts our spirits keep,
His presence bestows a calming grace.
Dispelling fear, leaving not a trace.

The Divine Justice
With Damaru's beat and Trishul's might,
He sets the scales of justice right.
For those who stray from the dharma's path,
He brings the karmic aftermath.

The Canine Sovereign
His faithful vahana, swift and keen,
A pack of dogs, a loyal scene,
They safeguard his shrines, both day and night.
Symbols of wisdom, pure and radiant.

The Liberator of Souls
From worldly bonds and earthly ties,
He helps the seeking soul to rise.
Through trials faced and lessons learned,
Salvation's path, by him discerned.

The Auspicious Destroyer
Though fierce his form, his purpose pure,
To cleanse the old, the new ensure.
An auspicious force, a potent sway,
Oh, Bhairava, we humbly bow and pray.

53

A Holy Fire: Dance of Divine Delight

Upon the hills where shadows dance and play,
Annamalai speaks, the sacred place to stay.
With peaks that touch the azure sky so bright,
The heart of Tamil land, a realm of light.

In ancient times, when myths were born anew,
Amidst the forests deep, the legends grew.
A steadfast deity, whose grace ignites,
Annamalaiyar, guide in darkest nights.

His matted locks, like flowing rivers bold,
Adorned with sacred ash, a sight to behold.
The sun would rise and dip, but never fade,
In his presence, all fears and doubts would wade.

With worshippers in throngs, his temple stands,
A beacon of solace, where faith expands.
A holy fire, Agni's strength, burns high,
Chanting echoes of a truth that never dies.

With every step upon this hallowed ground,
Devotees share stories, lost yet found.
The tales of love, of loss, of life so grand,
An endless tapestry, in which they stand.

Oh, mighty Lord, who opened galaxy doors,
With trembling hands, we cast our humble oars.
Beneath your gaze, the soul finds its release,
In silence, hearts entwine, and spirits cease.

Through stormy nights, when trials harshly press,
Your light, a guide, delivers from distress.
The wisdom in your gaze, a cooling balm,
And storms of life are hushed beneath your calm.

In the cool dusk, as stars begin to gleam,
The stories flow as if caught in a dream.
Of brazen warriors and the love, they pledged,
Of mothers' tears and hope that never edged.

The mountains whisper songs of ages past,
Of unity and strength that holds steadfast.
With every prayer, the air is thick with grace,
As Annamalaiyar blesses every face.

Oft do the rivers carve their ancient way,
Like paths of fate, where shadows often sway.
By your grace, we wander, bold and free,
Embracing life, its beauty, and its plea.

When devotees with flowers seek your vow,
Their hearts are aflame before your sacred brow.
Each petal laid, a symbol of their need,
In return, you nurture every hopeful seed.

Let the winds of Tamil lands proclaim,
The glory of your love, the eternal flame.
In every corner, from the mountain to the sea,
Your strength, O Lord, will ever stay with me.

54

Awakening the Inner Fire: Arunachala's Embrace

From Arunachala's heart, a fire blooms,
Annamalaiyar dispelling all the glooms.
A mountain silent, yet a voice profound,
Where truth and grace are ever to be found.

No form defined, yet felt in every breeze,
A cosmic presence, putting minds at ease.
The sacred flame, a beacon in the night,
A guide to freedom, bathed in holy light.

Through ancient caves and temples carved in stone,
His devotees whisper, never quite alone.
A pilgrimage inward, a burning, deep desire,
To merge with self and feel the sacred fire.

The Karthigai Deepam, a sky-embracing flare,
A symbol potent, banishing despair.
Annamalaiyar, in stillness, you abide,
The source of being, where all truths reside.

Let us climb, with open hearts and souls,
Towards the summit, reaching for our goals.
And in that silence, find the answering call,
Annamalaiyar, enfolding one and all.

55

The Call of Sonagiri: Unveiling Layers, Unfolding Lives

Upon the wings of morning,
The sun spills golden light,
Brushing the sacred Sonagiri hill,
Where ancient stones hold whispered tales.

Emerald cloaks drape the hillside,
A labyrinth of leafy tendrils,
Where the wind dances,
A playful spirit weaving laughter.

Here, the horizon melts,
As if kissed by dawn's soft breath,
And shadows stretch and yawn,
Across the humble earth.

Cacti rise like guardians,
Arms outstretched to the azure,
While wildflowers bloom in patches,
Their colours are a silent prayer.

Echoes of footsteps linger,
The soft crunch of gravel beneath,
Each step is a note in history's song,
Resonating through the undulating earth.

In the heart of the hill,
Ancient shrines stand resolute,
Carved from the very bones of the hill,
A testament of faith and devotion.

Marigolds nod in a gentle breeze,
Their radiance was a spark of joy,
While incense wafts from offerings laid,
An aroma that celebrates the divine.

The stillness is profound,
Broken only by the call of a distant bird,
Its song is a melody entwined,
With the murmur of prayerful thoughts.

Underneath the twisted banyan,
The earth exudes a quiet wisdom,
Roots like fingers tracing stories,
Etched in time, whispered by the wind.

Sacred, indeed, is this sanctuary,
Where spirits align with the sun,
And souls wander in reflection,
Lost yet found in quiet devotion.

At dusk, when the sky blushes,
The landscape transforms,
Fiery hues melt into twilight,
As stars begin their nightly odyssey.

Fingers of light weave through branches,
As the moon, a watchful guardian,
Drapes the hill in silver,
Seeking the sacred in every shadow.

The cool breeze carries secrets,
Of those who walked this path before,
Their stories etched in the very air,
A tapestry of lives interwoven.

Crickets chirp a nightly hymn,
A chorus to the ethereal dance,
As the hill breathes a sigh of content,
Cradling the dreams that linger long.

In the heart of this hallowed ground,
Resonates a truth most profound,
That all who walk upon this slope,
Are bound by the thread of sacred hope.

Let the winds carry our prayers,
Through valleys embraced by fragrant blooms,
For in the whispers of Sonagiri's breeze,
Lie the echoes of our love and devotion.

And when the day at last concludes,
And twilight blankets the sacred stone,
Let every heart find solace here,
Knowing that love resides within.

A journey eternal, a sacred pilgrimage,
Each breath intertwined with nature's song,
The sacred Sonagiri hill, a cherished place,
Where the spirit of the earth sings long.

56

Live in the Present Moment: Pure and Free

Beneath the gaze of Arunachala's peak,
Where ancient wisdom whispers, soft and meek,
Lies Sri Ramanasramam, a sanctuary still,
A haven in the heart, a balm to fill
The emptiness that shadows worldly strife,
A gentle pathway to a deeper life.

The air is thick with silence, charged and deep,
A promise whispered secrets it will keep.
Within the hall, the Master's presence lingers,
A resonance that time itself unhinges.
No grand pronouncements, no elaborate creed,
Just silent knowing, planting wisdom's seed.

The squirrels dart playfully among the trees,
The peacocks strut with elegant ease,
Unfettered by the questions that we bear,
Oblivious to the burdens that we share.
They live in the present moment, pure and free,
A lesson whispered for you and me.

To ponder "Who am I?" the constant call,
To shed the ego, watch the false self-fall.
To trace the source from whence the 'I' arose,

And find the peace that eternally bestows.
Its grace upon the seeker, weary and worn,
A homecoming awaited, long forlorn.

The chanting rises, a melodic stream,
Washing away the fragmented, waking dream.
The scent of incense, sweet and ever near,
Dispelling shadows, calming every fear.
The devotees gather, seeking solace there,
To lay their burdens down in silent prayer.

From every corner, hearts begin to mend,
As worldly attachments slowly transcend.
The mountain's power, palpable and vast,
A grounding presence, holding firm and fast.
It witnesses the struggles, hears the pleas,
And offers solace in the gentle breeze.

So come, dear traveller, if your soul is tired,
If worldly pursuits have left you uninspired.
Seek Ramanasramam, Arunachala's grace,
And find the Self reflected in this sacred place.
For in surrender, true freedom can be found,
Where the 'I' dissolves, and peace is profoundly crowned.

57

Grace of Wisdom:
In the Presence of Sri Ramana

Beneath the branches of venerable trees,
Where murmurs sway on fragrant zephyrs,
A sage, in quietude, profound and wise,
Rouses spirits from their restless slumber.

With eyes that encompass the infinite skies,
Reflecting the heart's hidden truths,
Sri Ramana, with the grace of wisdom,
Calls us to discover our authentic selves.

In the tranquillity, shadows dissipate,
Each thought dissolves, liberating the spirit,
"Who am I?" he softly inquires,
Revealing the truth through simple endeavours.

The mountains resonate with his tranquil melody,
In every heartbeat, joy intertwined with sorrow,
Yet through the veil of transient moments,
A glimpse of love, a vision divine.

Words flow like rivers, untainted and clear,
Inviting the seeker, enticing the uncertain,
"In your depths, the universe awaits,
Beyond thought, transcending the mind."

With each gaze, he nurtures illumination,
In the depths of darkness, a guiding presence,
His laughter, gentle yet resonant,
A soothing balm for wounds, a refuge for fear.

Oh, Sri Ramana, ageless sage,
Transform the restless into the wise;
Your presence, akin to a radiant dawn,
Awakens hearts to limitless brilliance.

Thus, allow me to dwell in your serene realm,
Where the ego dissolves, and fears vanish,
In the embrace of the eternal present,
With every breath, I humbly submit.

58

The King of the Heavens: Indra Lingam

In the heaven's embrace, where thunderous might lie,
Dwells the Indra Lingam, beneath vast, sprawling skies.
A ruler of realms, of the storms and the rain,
He wields both the tempest and a joy that breaks the chains.

Crafted from lightning, from cosmic decree,
He dances in thunder, bringing harmony.
The king of the heavens, in splendour and pride,
In the heart of creation, where forces collide.

With the strength of a thousand, yet gentle at hand,
Indra's spirit awakens a divine command.
In the showers of blessings, he nurtures the earth,
The cycles of seasons, the magic of birth.

Through trials and battles, his valour shines bright,
In the face of the darkness, he brings forth the light.
A reminder of balance, of might, woven deep,
In the tapestry woven, where heavens do weep.

For in every raindrop that kisses the ground,
The whispers of Indra in soft rhythms were found.
He teaches unity, power and grace,
In the thunder's deep rumble, we find our place.

So let us honour the storms that we weather,
For in their fierce dance, we find strength together.
In the heart of Indra, in power and peace,
We embrace our courage, as fears find release.

59

Luminescent Lore: Surya Lingam

In the dawn's golden cradle, where shadows retreat,
Dwells the Surya Lingam, where warmth and light meet.
A beacon of radiance, a flame in the sky,
It whispers of life as the sun starts to rise.

With every bright morning, it kindles the day,
Casting hopes on the horizon, chasing the darkness away.
In the dance of the sunbeams, in the brilliance so vast,
The Surya Lingam shines, a glow unsurpassed.

It carries the essence of strength and might,
In the pulse of creation, it ignites the pure light.
From the fiery heat to the cool morning dew,
Every ray speaks a promise, a living truth.

With colours of amber, saffron, and gold,
It entwines with the heavens, a story retold.
In the warmth of its laughter, our spirits ignite,
In the embrace of Surya, we bask in delight.

Guide us, O radiant, through struggles and strife,
Illuminate paths with the essence of life.
In the circle of seasons, through rise and decline,
We find in your presence a power divine.

As dusk paints the canvas and stars start to gleam,
We honour the sun in each heartfelt dream.
For in every sunrise, our souls' journey sings,
In the heart of the Surya, eternal joy springs

60

Dark Embrace: Yama Lingam

In the twilight of knowing, where silence is spun,
Dwells the Yama Lingam, with shadows begun.
A keeper of balance, both ending and start,
It weaves through the fabric of time and the heart.

With whispers of dusk, and the grace of the pall,
It teaches us lessons in the rise and in the fall.
In the stillness of twilight, where choices reside,
The Yama Lingam beckons, a guide at our side.

In the dance of the fates, both gentle and stern,
It cradles the flames of the lessons we learn.
With eyes like the cosmos, profound,
It echoes the truths in the cycle unbound.

Not just a bringer of endings, but also peace,
In surrender to waning, we find sweet release.
For in every closure, a new door awaits,
In the quiet of passing, life recalibrates.

Embrace the still moments, let go of the strife,
In the shadows of Yama, we honour our life.
With every heartbeat, in breaths softly drawn,
We embrace the eternal, the dusk and the dawn.

Let us remember, as we walk this tightrope,
That Yama's embrace holds the seeds of our hope.
In the heart of the lingam, where endings conjoin,
We find the essence of life, infinitely rejoined.

61

The Domain of the Earth: Niruthi's Lingam Chronicles

In the stillness of shadows, where silence reveals,
Resides the Niruthi Lingam, embodying wisdom concealed.
A domain of the earth, characterized by stability and grace,
It encompasses the essence of time, our hallowed space.

Under the expansive skies and the depths beneath,
It fosters the spirit within the flowing currents.
The core of the mountains, the resilience of stone,
In the sanctuary of Niruthi, we are never alone.

Robust and ageless, a sage of great insight,
It speaks of equilibrium as seasons take flight.
Within the profound wisdom of nature's founding,
We discover our reflections, leading to rejuvenation.

With each tender caress of the earth, we rise,
In the subterranean depths, old wounds begin to heal.
The serene grounding, so invaluable, so rare,
In the essence of the lingam, we relinquish our burdens.

From the quakes of the earth to the shimmer of stars,
Niruthi reminds us of our closeness.
From the essence of existence to the rhythm of the soil,
In its tranquil embrace, our authentic selves are revealed.

Thus, allow your heart to anchor, let your spirit soar,
In the timeless presence of unity's call.
For in every heartbeat, through each gentle resonance,
We reflect the wisdom of the Niruthi Lingam.

62

Whispers of the Wind: Varuna Lingam

From boundless heavens, where the rains commence to fall,
A deity emerges from the profound depths of the sea.
Varuna, the embodiment of ocean, sky, and tide,
Where mystical currents flow within his very being.

Yet the earth takes shape, cloaked in shadows, cool and grey,
A Lingam ascends, in a manner most sacred.
More than a mere phallus, it symbolizes the cosmos,
Representing powerful forces, intertwined and divine.

Varuna's waters will cascade over stone,
A perpetual blessing, displayed in gentle grace.
The formless essence, moulded into earthly form,
A tale softly spoken, waiting through the ages to be revealed.

Consider this depiction, profound and tranquil,
Where the essence of water converges with the earth's steadfast
    resolve.
The infinite sea, exhibiting a refined elegance,
Divinity unveiled, transcending time and space.

Varuna Lingam, a timeless enigma,
Where the waters murmur of everlastingness.
A quiet strength, preserved within the stone,
The universal rhythm, intertwining body and spirit.

175

63

Breath Beneath the Stone: Vayu Lingam

Beneath the branches of venerable trees,
Where murmurs glide on a fragrant breeze,
A sage, in quietude, profound and wise,
Stirs the spirits from their slumbering ties.

With eyes that reflect the boundless skies,
A mirror revealing the heart's disguise,
Sri Ramana, with the grace of insight,
Guides us toward our most authentic light.

In the tranquillity, shadows dissipate,
In the breath of the cosmos, where whispers elevate,
Resides the Vayu Lingam, in the play of the glow.
A spirit of air, with a touch so divine,

With each gentle breeze, secrets are woven,
Echoes of joy where earthly hearts are driven.
In the rustling leaves, in the ocean's sigh,
The Vayu Lingam calls, come, heed my cry.

It is the murmur of freedom in expansive skies,
The surge of the currents, where the spirit will rise.
In the tender embrace of the cool night air,
Breath of the sacred, we discover solace there.

From peaks to valleys, it courses through the land,
A reminder of motion, of life, and hand.
It embodies both change and constancy, a lesson learned,
In the essence of the wind, our deepest desires burned.

As we sing to the breezes, our souls reclaim,
In the dance of the Vayu, we are reborn again.
For within every gust lie dreams yet untold,
In the embrace of the wind, we find the bold.

Thus, open your spirit, let the currents entwine,
In the presence of Vayu, no limits, no lines.
For the breath of creation will resonate through us all,
In this expanse of movement, we heed the call.

64

Mysteries Wrapped in Golden Dust: Kubera Lingam

In the realm of abundance, where fortune bestows,
Dwells the Kubera Lingam, where prosperity grows.
A symbol of riches, of treasures untold,
It cradles the dreams of warm hearts and souls.

With golden vibrations, it sings with delight,
In the shimmer of wealth under soft, radiant light.
A guardian of riches, both spiritual and grand,
Kubera, the wealth-holder, with blessings at hand.

In the depths of our yearning, its essence ignites,
In the dance of our fortunes, in luminous nights.
With every whispered prayer, with each heartfelt call,
It opens the gateways, inviting them all.

Not merely of gold or the glittering sheen,
But of love's vibrant currency, of joy evergreen.
In the sharing of kindness, in laughter, in care,
This lingam teaches riches beyond compare.

Through trials and journeys, as paths intertwine,
Kubera's embrace brings a bounty divine.
In every small gesture, in gratitude sowed,
We discover the treasures that true life bestows.

Let us remember, as we walk this fine line,
That wealth is a river, ever flowing and kind.
In the heart of the Kubera, in abundance of grace,
We find the true riches in love's warm embrace.

65

Intersection of Time and Space: The Elusive Esanya Lingam

Esanya Lingam, a name softly spoken,
A stone's embodiment, a delicate spark.
A journey begins towards the northeast's embrace,
Within a hallowed realm, at the intersection of time and space.

The form of a Lingam, polished and frigid,
Yet it carries tales from epochs long past.
Esanya's presence, a gentle mentor,
Where wisdom flows freely, and truths are revealed.

It may arise as a pillar, reaching for the heavens,
Into the boundless expanse of the azure sky.
Or it may rest quietly, at the core of a temple,
Resonating with a mystical vibration, heralding a new beginning.

It conveys the essence of angles and unseen lines,
Where energies gather and intertwine.
In the harmony discovered, and forces that unite,
Lies are a silent strength that remains unforgettable.

Esanya Lingam, within the consciousness,
A notion subtle, elusive to grasp.
Yet within these verses, an echo persists,
Of ancient journeys and revered traditions.

66

Sorrow's Serenade: Ballads from the Broken Soul

In stillness deep, where whispers cease to be,
A potent force, for all the world to see.

No booming voice, no crashing cymbal's sound,
Yet a deafening presence fills the space around.

A vacant room, where echoes fail to bloom,
A heavy cloak that seals a spirit's doom.

The lover's quarrel, ending not in strife,
But frozen gaze, that cuts into the life.

A friendship frayed, no harsh words left to sting,
Just a hollow space, where laughter used to sing.

The absent father, never there to guide,
A silent void, where love and trust have died.

The battlefield, when cannon fire is done,
A silent tomb beneath the setting sun.

The artist's block, when inspiration's flown,
A canvas stark, where creativity's unknown.

The student's mind, when understanding is lost,
A silent plea, at overwhelming cost.

The aging soul, as senses start to wane,
A quiet world, a growing, lonely pain.

The ocean's depths, where sunlight cannot reach,
A silent realm, beyond our mortal speech.

A sleeping forest, blanketed in snow,
A hushed domain, where secrets softly grow.

The moment's pause, before the storm breaks free,
A silent threat, for all the world to see.

For in the silence, truths begin to rise,
Reflections born within our very eyes.

67

Flames Beneath the Fog: A Pilgrim's Perplexing Path

Where earth ascends to kiss the heaven's grace,
Stands Annamalai, a sacred, stony face.
A silent sentinel, in ageless sleep,
Whose ancient secrets, devotees keep.
A mountain mystic, draped in hues of dawn,
Awaits the moment when the night is gone.

Then, from its peak, a beacon bursts alight,
Annamalai Deepam, banishing the night.
A fiery promise, painted on the sky,
A golden answer to a fervent sigh.
The ghee-fed flames dance and twist and leap,
A silent language, secrets buried deep.

For generations, pilgrims gather near,
Drawn by the brilliance, casting out all fear.
Their hearts are ablaze with longing, pure and true,
To merge within the light and be made new.
They chant the sacred names, a rhythmic plea,
For liberation, from life's decree.

The mountain echoes with the fervent sound,
As ashes whisper from the hallowed ground.
A transformation was witnessed in the blaze,
Where ego crumbles in the fiery haze.
Each devotee, a spark within the whole,
Surrenders burdens and reclaims their soul.

This light kindle something deep inside,
A knowing silence, where true peace can hide.
It speaks of oneness, beyond form and name,
A universal truth, an eternal flame.
Let us gaze upon this sacred sight,
And find within ourselves, Annamalai's Light.

68

A Love Story: Whispered Beneath the Skies

In Arunachala's shadow, grand and deep,
Where sacred mountain secrets softly sleep,
Stands Arunachaleshwara, Shiva's light,
Eternally burning, a beacon bright.

He is the fire, the formless, vast, and old,
A story whispered legends to be told.
He is the stillness, the silence, knowing gaze,
Reflecting the soul in countless ways.

And by His side, a source of gentle grace,
Mother Unnamulai, in this hallowed place.
She is the Shakti, the power, life's embrace,
The Mother Goddess, filling time and space.

She is the nurturer, the compassion deep,
Where weary spirits find solace and sleep.
She is the wisdom, the intuitive guide,
Leading lost pilgrims to Shiva's side.

He is the mountain, steadfast and serene.
She is the river, flowing evergreen.
He is the silence, profound and ever near,
She is the mantra, banishing all fear.

Within their union, a balance so divine,
The cosmic dance, eternally entwined.
Lord Arunachaleshwarar and Mother Unnamulai,
A love story whispered beneath the sky.

69

Harmony in Hushed Space: Finding My Voice

The world explodes with clamour, a cacophony untold,
Yet silence screams the loudest, a story to unfold.

A hush that falls like snowfall on fields of bustling sound,
A pregnant pause of meaning, profoundly all around.

The absence of a sentence, a question left unasked,
A truth too raw and painful, beneath a careful mask.

A lover's fight concluded with slammed and heavy doors,
The echoing reverberation of unspoken, aching sores.

The memory of laughter, in a house now standing still,
A phantom of a chorus, upon a lonely hill.

The missing voice of guidance, a comfort no more near,
A vacant space where wisdom, once banished, every fear.

The artist's final canvas, incomplete and left behind,
A whispered, silent promise of genius yet to find.

The earth's soft, muted breathing, before a raging storm,
A quiet, tense anticipation of nature's brutal form.

The moment just before sleep, when thoughts begin to fade,
A silent, vast expansion, where memories are made.

The understanding shared between two souls entwined,
A language past all speaking, a treasure for the mind.

The blank page waits for stories, a universe untold,
A silent, fertile promise of narratives of old.

So, listen to the silence; its secrets it will keep,
The loudest of all voices lull the world to sleep.

70

Embers of Tomorrows: Light Up the Lost Pathways

The world is hushed, asleep.
Dreams unfolding like a rose.
Petals gently swaying slowly
As the wind carries scents of blooming flowers
Fragrant as the morning dews.

But in this quiet hour of rest
Lies a beauty that's hard to find
In the silence, hearts can hear.
The whispers of their deepest fears
And the love that they've been bound.

Yet in the darkness, there's a light.
A gentle glow that shines so bright.
Guiding those who wander lost
Through life's uncertain, winding roads,
Toward a path that's yet unknown.

Let us cherish every moment.
And let the peace of night descend.
Upon our souls, a balm that heals
Wounds of time, and calms the heart.
Bringing solace to what we feel.

71

Mindscapes: Illuminating the Shadows of Sri Ramanasramam

In the heart of the hills where silence sings,
Where time droops low on twilight's wings,
Amidst the boughs where the sacred pulse beats,
There lies a haven where the spirit meets.

Amidst the shadows of Banyan trees,
With whispers carried on the melodious breeze,
In every leaf, a tale unfolds,
In every stone, a secret is held.

The sacred hall, a temple of grace,
Where seekers gather, each face a trace,
Of longing deep, of yearning pure,
In this stillness, souls find a cure.

He, the sage with eyes that see,
Beyond the bounds of you and me,
With words like rivers, flowing wide,
Through valleys of doubt, he becomes our guide.

Oh, Ramanasramam, your sacred grounds,
Where echoes of truth in silence resound,
The laughter of children, the prayerful song,
A symphony where all hearts belong.

The gentle sun dips and sways,
As twilight dances in soft, golden rays,
And the mountains, still, wear a cloak of grace,
Each moment in this refuge is a warm embrace.

In the chants of peace, in the rustling leaves,
The spirit awakens, the heart believes,
For here in this sanctuary, minds can roam,
Finding in stillness that deep inner home.

Roots that Reach:
Sri Dakshina Murthy's Embrace

In the silent whisper of the ancient tree,
Is heard the wisdom of Sri Dakshina Murthy's grace.
With roots that delve into eternity,
His teachings spread a timeless, boundless space.

Upon his brow, the crescent moon does rest,
A symbol of eternal light and a guide.
The symbols on his form, though subtle, attest
To know the vast seas where truths reside.

Beneath the banyan's canopy where shadows play,
He remains in stillness; time cannot confine him.
His disciples gather near to hear him say,
The secrets are concealed in each sacred sign.

In silence deep, his teachings flow like springs,
Nourishing intellects with each subtle sound.
And as he speaks, an inner peace he brings;
A harmony within our hearts is found.

Awakening Within: The Empowering Echoes of Sri Ramana's Silence

Beneath the boughs of ancient trees,
Where whispers dance on the fragrant breeze,
A sage in silence, profound and deep,
Awakens souls from restless sleep.

With eyes that hold the vastest skies,
A mirror to the heart's disguise,
Sri Ramana, with wisdom's grace,
Invites us to our truest place.

In the stillness, shadows flee,
Each thought dissolves, sets the spirit free,
"Who am I?" he gently asks,
Unveiling the truth in simple tasks.

The mountains echo his serene refrain,
In every heartbeat, joy and pain,
Yet through the veil of fleeting time,
A glance at love, a glimpse sublime.

Words like rivers, flowing pure,
Invite the seeker, tempt the unsure,
"In your depths, the world you'll find,
Beyond the thought, beyond the mind."

With every look, he cradles light,
In the depths of darkness, a guiding sight,
His laughter ringing, soft yet clear,
A balm for wounds, a home for fear.

Oh, Sri Ramana, timeless sage,
Turn the restless into the sage;
Your presence is like a sunrise bright,
Awakens hearts to boundless light.

Allow me to sit in your silent space,
Where the ego melts, and fears erase,
In the embrace of the eternal now,
With every breath, I humbly bow.

Beneath the Surface:
Words Drown in Despair

The atmosphere weighs heavily, thick with inept sorrows,
A tension rising, stoking primitive fears.
No quiver disrupts the voice, no cry escapes,
Only frozen, quiet in these empty forms.

A war of words unspoken and unacknowledged,
A silent storm gathers within the chest.
The mouth, a deceiver, shackled by unseen bonds,
While fury surges within, in fiery blood.

No rumbling thunder, no explosion,
Just quiet anguish, resonating from history.
A gulf yawns, broader than the heavens,
Mirroring torment that refuses to fade.

For sound can comfort, and words can heal the fracture,
But silence festers, for heaven's sake.
It cultivates bitterness, tainting all that's pure,
A gradual decline that's endlessly certain.

Serenity's Serenade: A Toast to Inner Bliss

The world clamours, a chaotic din,
A constant rush, a battle to win.
Voices rise, opinions clash,
In the tumultuous storm, spirits thrash.

Yet deep within, a quiet space,
A sanctuary, a peaceful place.
Where echoes fade and worries cease,
And weary souls can find release.

Quiet falls, a soothing touch,
To ease the soul and feel as such.
No need now to talk or strive,
Just allow the stillness to thrive.

For within this calm, a strength exists,
A source profound beyond the mist.
Where ideas can take root and prosper,
And bravery awakens from its slumber.

Stillness is not void,
But a rich soil for inner joy.
A source of powerful energy,
To lead us to the clearest light.

Thus, pursue the calm, valiant, and daring.
And allow its tale to remain unspoken.
For within the stillness, strength is discovered,
A tranquillity that mends the restless mind.

76

Cognitive Crescendo:
The Symphony of Self – Awareness

In twilight's hush, where shadows softly fall,
A quiet space for meditation's gentle call,
The mind awakens, free from the worldly din,
To find itself, its depths sink within.

The breath, a river, flowing calm and deep,
Echoes through the chambers of the soul to keep,
As thoughts arise, like clouds across the sky,
They pass, leaving room for clarity to sigh.

Within this stillness, like a lotus blooms bright,
Self-realization dawns, a radiant light,
That shines upon the heart and gently shows,
The paths we've trod, the choices that we know.

Through the introspection's lens, we see our past,
And with compassion, we forgive at last.
The fears and doubts that once did hold us tight,
Like autumn leaves, they rustle, then take flight.

The present moment stands, a canvas clear,
For painting life's masterpiece, without fear,
The future beckons, like a dawn's sweet song,
A chance to write the next chapter, strong.

With every breath, we rise above the pain.
And find our truest selves, no longer confined in vain,
Free to choose, to love, to live, to grow,
In harmony with nature, our hearts aglow.

In meditation's silence, we discover who we are,
A spark of divinity, shining near and far,
A reflection of the universe's design,
A drop of water, part of the ocean's shine.

The Silent Volcano: Who Am I?

Dust motes dancing.
Sunbeam shafts, thick silence.
A mountain breathes.

Arunachala.
Not a place, but a pulling,
A gravity deep.

(Am)

The question blooms
From bone and breath, a mantra
Unspoken, felt.

Who? A finger
Pointing back at the pointer,
The mirror shattered brightly.

(I?)

Words, a river
Eroding banks of knowing,
To oceans vast.

No self to find,
Only the emptying,
The boundless remains.

(Silence)

The heart's whisper.
A stillness that swallows sound.
Just Being remains.

The guru's gaze,
A bonfire of illusions,
Ashes softly fall.

(The Answer)

Not an answer was found,
But the dissolving of self,
In the question's heat.

Ramana smiles,
A gentle, knowing echo:
"Be Still. Know Thyself."

(Arunachala)

Forever turning,
A silent, burning question,
Who Am I? Remains.

78

Echoes of Eternity:
Arunachala's Cryptic Chorus

(I)

Stone.
Just Stone?
No.

A hum.
Deep tectonic throat,
Chanting silence.

Rust and ochre bleed
Into sapphire sky,
A bruise of holiness.

(II)

Barefoot pilgrims,
Dust-kissed soles,
Trace the circumambulation.

Each step,
A prayer worn thin,
A mantra ground into granite.

The mountain breathes.
Inhale: devotion.
Exhale: eternity.

(III)

Caves whisper secrets,
Of Ramana, of stillness,
Of the Self unravelling.

The ego,
A dry leaf,
Caught in the updraft.

No summit sought.
Only the base,
The immutable core.

(IV)

Dogs bark prayers.
Crows circle wisdom.
Monkeys mirror madness.

All creatures,
Reflections of the ONE,
Dancing in the dust.

(V)

Sunrise.
A molten kiss,
On the face of the ancient.

Shadows shrink,
Doubt dissolves,
In the incandescent truth.

Arunachala.
Not a mountain,
But a magnet.

Pulling us
Home.
Always.

79

Mystic Murmurs Beneath Sacred Skies: The Allure of Arunachala

(I)

Burnt orange
Breath of rock face
Silence echoes
Upward.

A prayer, a cough, a rustle of leaves.

Sun-baked skin
Dreams of granite
Etched in faces
Knowing.

(II)

Shiva.
Unmoving.
All-moving.
The Axis Mundi.

A beggar's bowl reflects the infinite.

Shadow play
On ancient stone
Stories whispered
Alone.

(III)

Fire dances
In the heart's cave
A yearning burn
To rave.

The wind a mantra, unwritten, untold.

Dust devil's swirl
Around bare feet
A pilgrimage
Complete?

(IV)

No beginning
No ending found
Only presence
Profound.

The mountain sighs, a geological sigh.

Emptiness filled
With Shiva's grace
A timeless, still
Embrace.

(V)

(A single, echoing syllable)

OM.

80

Lunar Litanies: Chanting Hope Along Girivalam

Barefoot Prayer

Dust. Ochre grits kiss skin.
Sun bleeds. Noon, a hammer.
Each step is a syllable, an unsung mantra.
Arunachala. Arunachala.
Whispered echo in the skull's cathedral.

Stone Song

Granite shoulder, ancient, scarred.
Wind-etched stories only silence holds.
A lizard flicks a green lightning code.
This mountain breathes.
I feel it's cold, unyielding grace.
My story unfolds...or dissolves...

Street Symphony

Sandalwood and diesel fumes.
Beggar's bowl, a clinking moon.
Children's laughter, high-pitched tune.

Cowbell clang, a shifting dune of sound.
The spirit blooms,
A fragile, paper flower.

Shadow Play

Twilight descends. Arunachala,
A silhouette against the fiery sky.
The path, a ribbon, unwinding.
I am one with the countless, passing by.
A shared breath, a collective sigh.
Where do I begin?
Where do I die?

Third Eye Open (Maybe)

Stars ignite. The mountain sleeps.
But something stirs beneath the deep,
Rock heart.
A promise keeps,
A secret sown while the world weeps.
The turning world.
The endless steeps.
The turning.
The endless.

Aftermath

With each footfall, a prayer is released.
Each breath is a debt that's ceased.
The mountain stands, a silent priest.
And in my soul, a newfound peace...

Or just exhaustion...
Hard to say, the least.
But changed.
Undeniably, changed.

81

Heart Alight on Arunachala's Height: A Celestial Celebration

On sacred grounds, I pause and gaze,
Where mighty Arunachala's peak amazes,
A mountain revered by sages old,
In Tiruvannamalai, where legends abound.

With panchamukha and a mystic aura high,
It stands as a sentinel of the southern sky,
Bathed in the golden light of sunrise bright,
And painted pink with twilight's gentle night.

I take my first step, a pilgrim true,
Circumambulating this revered shrine anew,
The path unwinds like a serpent's sway,
As I walk clockwise, in devotion's holy way.

With each turn around the hill, I make with care,
Offering prayers and blessings to share,
For Sri Ramana's wisdom is pure and deep,
Echoes within my heart, in silent sleep.

The wind whispers secrets, ancient and wise,
As I tread the path, with open eyes,
The scent of incense wafts, a fragrant treat,
As I surrender, my soul skips a beat.

With each stride, I let go and find,
My true self, left behind,
Like autumn leaves that fall from trees so tall,
My ego's chains break and lose their hold on all.

The world recedes, and I behold,
Arunachala's splendour, young and old,
A beacon of love that shines so bright and free,
Leading me back home, where I am meant to be.

In this circular dance, I lose myself,
Yet uncover my genuine essence in this sacred wealth,
Of devotion, faith, and love divine,
That Arunachala embodies all the time.

Thus, I keep walking, round and round,
This mountain is sacred, forever bound,
To its teachings, its power and might,
Arunachala, glowing with beauty, in plain sight.

82

Sea of Souls: From the Skandasramam's Ancient Gates

The sun ascends, a fiery eye, on Annamalai's peak so high,
Arunachala, sacred name, a pilgrim's heart, aflame, aflame.

From Skandasramam's ancient gate, the pradakshina, we
    celebrate,
A sacred walk, a path divine, where earthly concerns cease to
    shine.

The devotees, a sea of souls, with hearts devout and spirits
    whole,
They circle around the holy hill, their whispered prayers filling
    the air,

Through bustling streets and quiet lanes, a tapestry of sights and
    strains,
The aroma of incense wafts in the breeze, gently rustling
    through the trees.

Past temples grand, and shrines so small, a history echoes
    through them all,
Of sages wise and gods revered, their tales softly are conferred.

The sun beats down, and the trek stretches long, yet faith and
   song bolster spirits strong.
Each step a prayer, each breath a supplication, to Arunachala,
   eternally.

The chanting swells, a swelling tide of love and peace that
   cannot conceal,
A vibrant hum, a sacred sound, as holy ground is hallowed
   ground.

At sunset's embrace, the mountain glows, a fiery heart, its
   beauty shows,
A million hues, a painted scene, a wondrous sight, serene.

Then, as darkness falls, the stars ignite, a million lamps burn
   ever bright,
The pradakshina end draws near, with grateful hearts and spirits
   clear.

Around the hill, the pilgrimage concludes, a sacred journey
   beneath the sun.
Arunachala, ever bright, a beacon shining, pure and light.

83

Morning Light, Midnight Delight:
The Radiance of Arunachala

In the realms where the sun gently graces the dawn,
Lies Arunachala, majestic and drawn,
A beacon of light in the core of the earth,
Where seekers of truth in devotion do stand.

With bare feet and a spirit unbound,
Pilgrims gather, enveloped in wonderment,
The hallowed trail curling in a snug embrace,
Where the shadows of sages caress the calm night.

Each stone narrates a tale, every footstep a plea,
As murmurs of insight linger in the breeze,
The hills raise their voices, an anthem of the heart,
The rhythms of many, in harmony, part.

Oh, Arunachala, your splendour gleams bright,
In the quiet of morning, in the depths of night,
The flames of surrender dance high in the air,
As the moon drapes her silver on the mountains laid bare.

With offerings of flowers and songs from the heart,
The devotees gather, never to part,
In quietude they wander, in laughter they roam,
The circle of love, where all feel at home.

The echoed chants rise like incense in flight,
Binding each seeker to truth and light,
Through valleys of despair, through summits of bliss,
Each step is a voyage; each breath is a ploy.

Thus, they continue on this sacred Giri.
Bathed in the sun's warmth, where worries grow few,
For Arunachala cradles each soul with such grace,
In the hills' heart, they discover their place.

சிவ சிவ

84

Illuminated Identities: Finding Self from the Sacred Fire

Upon the sacred heights of Annamalai, a radiant beacon shines,
Karthikai Deepam, a revered light, an ancient mystical vision.
The mountain rises, a bold giant, against the twilight sky,
Where tales of bygone eras dwell, folded in whispered myth.

From far and wide, pilgrims arrive, with hearts sincere and true,
To behold this divine glow, a sight eternally fresh.
For on this night, the holy fire climbs to the heights above,
A representation of the Lord's mighty name, connecting earth and sky.

The air is heavy with sweet incense, and mantras fill the night.
As numerous feet on dusty paths share a sacred journey.
The Arunachaleshwara's blessing, upon the devoted descends,
A serene smile on every visage, within the holy temple's embrace.

The sun descends, a glowing orb, behind the distant hills,
As shadows stretch, dark and tall, the sacred mountain awakens.
Then, from the summit, a sudden flare brightens the night.
A towering flame's fervent glow, a breathtaking, magnificent sight.

A lone flame, a powerful spark, breaking earthly confines,
A guiding light piercing the darkness on this consecrated ground.
It embodies hope, it embodies faith, a boundless love,
Cleansing away all worldly strife, a blessing to elevate.

The faithful gaze; their spirits lift, their hearts filled with joy.
As the sacred tale of Karthikai Deepam eternally holds significance.
A moment engraved, a vivid image, a time to cherish,
The mountain's radiance, a holy beacon, upon Annamalai's countenance.

85

The Cosmic Dance: From Ashes
to Enlightenment

From primal chaos, Shiva's might unfurl,
A cosmic dance, where the universe swirls.
Creation's breath, destruction's fiery hand,
A lord of lords, across the shifting sand.
But in his heart, a mystery resides,
A power deeper, where the knowledge hides.

For Shiva, strong, with matted locks so wild,
Possessed a half, a gentler, softer child.
Parvati, Shakti, Goddess of the Dawn,
Her love, a flame, would brightly be born.
Their union blessed, a sacred, holy deed,
A merging soul, a planted cosmic seed.

From Shiva's strength and Parvati's grace,
A form arose in time and space.
Ardhanarishwarar, half of each divine
A perfect blend, forever intertwined.
One body shared, a mirrored, mystic sight,
The masculine, the feminine, alight.

The sunlit side, a Shiva's strength untold,
The crescent moon, a Parvati's embrace of old.
On one side, a trident, fierce and bold,
The other, gentle stories to unfold.
A single face, with eyes that deeply see,
Reflecting worlds, eternity.

For in this form, a deep lesson takes hold,
Of balance found, a story is to be told.
That strength and grace are not opposed, but one,
A woven tapestry beneath the setting sun.
The masculine, the feminine, entwined as one,
In perfect harmony, their journey began.

The demons raged in fear and dark despair,
At such a power, beyond compare.
They sought to break the bond so strong and true,
But Ardhanarishwarar saw their wicked hue.
With grace and might, the darkness they defied,
And banished the evil, far and wide.

The sages watched, with wisdom's knowing gaze,
At Ardhanarishwara's enlightening blaze.
The scriptures sung of this divine embrace,
A symbol sacred, of love's time and space.
A potent image, for all souls to see,
The wholeness found in unity.

Through ages past, the legend lives anew,
A testament to love forever true.
Ardhanarishwarar, a guiding light so bright,

A beacon shining in the darkest night.
A reminder that in balance, strength we find,
A merging of the body and the mind.

Let us strive to live in harmony's grace,
Reflecting love, in every time and space.
To find the balance, in our earthly way,
And emulate the Ardhanarishwara's sway.
For in that union, true strength will reside,
A gentle power, a love that cannot hide.

86

Chasing Shadows: The Lost Verses of Lord Pichandavar

The Wandering Mendicant
With ash-smeared body, simple guise,
A begging bowl beneath the skies,
Lord Pichandavar, he roams free,
A symbol of humility.

The Lord of Detachment
From worldly ties and earthly gain,
He turns away, untouched by pain,
A master of renunciation's art,
Dwelling within the devotee's heart.

The Playful Wanderer
With a gentle smile and carefree gait,
He wanders through the cosmic state,
A playful form of the divine,
Whose presence makes our spirits shine.

The Companion of Canines
Surrounded by his loyal band,
The dogs that follow, paw in the sand,
Symbolizing unwavering faith,
Guiding us through the journey of life and death.

The Destroyer of Ego
The skull he holds is a stark display,
Of ego's end, its swift decay,
A reminder that all must cease,
And find true liberation's peace.

The Giver of Alms
Though he appears to seek our share,
It is our pride he desires to bear,
By offering all, we understand,
The boundless grace of his command.

The Embodiment of Simplicity
No grand adornments, jewels so bright,
His beauty lies in inner light,
Lord Pichandavar, a humble plea,
To bestow upon us genuine simplicity.

87

In the Mirror of Ardhanarishwara: Reflection of Love and Destruction

Through mountains tall and rivers wide,
In the forest deep where shadows hide,
The spirit danced, the essence flowed,
In every creature, love is bestowed.

Oh, ardent lord of wisdom deep,
In meditation, secrets keep,
With crescent moon upon thy brow,
You guide the lost in solemn vow.

The demon was dark with shadowed breath,
Stalked 'midst the realms, a herald of death,
Yet fearless stood the fused divine,
With a vibrant heart and purpose fine.

From ashes, rose their sacred fire,
To forge a path, to lift, inspire,
With trident held, and lotus bloom,
They cast aside the creeping gloom.

In battle fierce, with thunder's roar,
They struck the ground, the heavens bore,
The dance of cosmic energies played,
In every clash, life's mystery laid.

Oh, Ardhanarishwarar, essence pure,
Symbol of love, hope, demure,
In you, the cycles intertwine,
Of birth, of death, in sacred line.

As nature sways, to rhythms slow,
In every heart where love shall grow,
You teach the world to harmonize,
To seek the truth beyond the lies.

The clouds adorned in sunlit grace,
Reflect the union, bright embrace,
In every heartbeat, every sigh,
The spirit sings, it cannot lie.

So, let the tale through the ages ring,
Of Ardhanarishwarar, the cosmic king,
In unity, we all shall stand,
To weave the magic, hand in hand.

In silence deep and vibrant cheer,
Your presence whispers, always near,
For in this dance of life and strife,
We find the spark, the breath of life.

Rejoice, O seekers, in the light,
Of duality, pure and bright,
For in our hearts, this truth resides,
In Ardhanarishvara, love abides.

Now legends weave through time and space,
In the hearts of many, we find our place,
With every step, through joy and pain,
Let love unite, like sun and rain.

An epic was sung in lands afar,
Of Shiva's peace and Parvati's star,
Together as one, they rule the night,
In harmony, we find our sight.

88

Sorrow's Serenade:
Ballads from the Broken Soul

In the quiet of the night, I feel so lost,
Whispers of my heart come at a cost.

Memories like shadows follow me near,
Who am I in your absence? The answer is clear.

Days pass like pages turning so fast,
Each moment is a reminder of a love that won't last.

I seek a grin in the mirror, frigid sheen,
But all I find is a heart swollen with longing.

Laughter once danced in the warmth of your light,
Now silence surrounds me like a starless night.

I reach for your hand, but it's gone from my grasp,
Each breath feels heavy, each moment a gasp.

Dreams that we painted are fading away,
The hues of our past are now turning grey.

I wander this world with a heart full of ache,
Who am I without you? Just a soul left to break.

Yet amidst my grief, a glimmer persists,
A belief that someday love will shatter these chains.

Although the journey feels lonely and the road unkind,
I'll cherish your memory forever intertwined.

89

Identity's Labyrinth:
Where Beginnings Meet Endings

In twilight's hush, where shadows softly fall,
A sage did sit, beyond them all,
Sri Ramana Maharshi, a mystic soul so bright,
Leading seekers to the truth of endless night.

His eyes aglow with wisdom's inner fire,
He taught that Self-Inquiry is the ultimate desire,
To turn within and search for what we are not,
And uncover the truth that lies beyond the thought's hot spot.

"Who am I?" he asked, his words like gentle rain,
Falling on hearts that sought to know again,
Their true nature concealed deep within their chest,
Where love and peace dwell, all burdens find rest.

The mind, a restless wanderer, ever on the roam,
Chasing desires, fears, and doubts, its home,
But Ramana showed us how to soothe it down,
And attune to the silence, in this sacred town.

Like lotus flowers blooming in the muddy stream,
We rise above the world's tumultuous dream,
Our ego, the snake that hisses at our ears,
Is tamed by the knowledge that "I am not here."

The three states of waking, dreaming, and sleep,
Are but a veil, a curtain to keep,
The reality from the view, of the Self, pure and bright,
That shines eternally, without a single light.

Ramana's teachings echoed through the ages-old,
A call to awaken, to let go, to unfold,
The petals of the heart, to reveal the rose so fair,
And find the bliss that lies beyond compare.

Through his words, we see the mirror of the mind,
Reflecting on all the thoughts that leave us blind,
The noise, the chatter, the constant din and fray,
Give way to silence, as the darkness fades away.

The journey inward, a path so steep and long,
Requires courage, patience, and a heart that's strong,
For in the depths of our being, lies the truth we seek,
A truth that sets us free, and makes our spirit speak.

Like a river flowing to the ocean's shore,
We merge with the infinite, forever more,
Our individuality, a drop that blends with the sea,
And in that union, we find eternity.

In Ramana's presence, we feel the energy high,
A vibration that resonates, and touches the sky,
A sense of unity, of oneness, we adore,
With all that exists, and forever explore.

The Self, the ultimate goal, the treasure so rare,
Lies hidden within, yet waiting there,
To be discovered, to be known, to be seen,
By those who dare to look, and have faith serene.

So let us follow Ramana's guiding light,
And walk the path, through the dark of night,
For in the stillness, we'll find our peaceful nest,
And in that silence, we'll be blessed.

The Self, the source, the beginning and the end,
The mystery that unfolds, as the story transcends,
Ramana's teachings echo, a timeless refrain,
Reminding us to look within, and find our way again.

As we breathe in, the air we inhale,
We become aware of our true nature's gale,
The wind that blows, the sun that shines so bright,
Are but reflections of the Self, our inner light.

In Ramana's footsteps, we take our stride,
Through the labyrinth of the mind, where thoughts reside,
Until we reach the centre, the hub of our wheel,
Where the Self, the axis, reveals itself, all too real.

The journey's long, but the destination is near,
A promise kept, a bond that's clear,
Between the seeker, and the truth they seek,
A bond of love, that will never speak.

In Ramana's light, we find our way,
Through the maze of life, come what may,
And when we finally arrive at the gate of gold,
We'll realize, that we've been home, all along, so bold.

The mystery solved, the riddle revealed,
The Self, the answer, that we've concealed,
In the depths of our being, where it resides,
A treasure trove, where love and peace abide.

And so, we remember, Ramana's gentle voice,
Whispering secrets, in a loving choice,
To turn within, to look within our heart,
And find the truth, that sets us apart.

This truth, a gift, a legacy so grand,
A treasure passed down, from hand to hand,
From Ramana's hand, to ours, a sacred trust,
To carry forward, and always rust.

May we honour him, this saint so divine,
Who showed us the way, to the Self's shrine,
And may his teachings guide us, every step of the way,
As we journey inward, to the dawn of day.

And when our time comes, and we depart,
May Ramana's blessing remain in our hearts,
A spark that guides us, to the other side,
Where love and peace await, with no goodbyes to hide.

In the realm of the Self, we're free to roam,
Where love and joy, are our eternal home,
Thanks to Ramana, who lit the way,
And guided us to the truth, night and day.

90

Echoes of Essence: In Muffed Moments

In mystic realms of thought and time,
A question echoes through my mind's chime,
Who am I? A query so profound,
A mystery that's shrouded all around.

I delve into my soul for answers deep,
But like a river's source, they seem to creep,
Out of view, yet concealed from my gaze,
Leaving me with uncertainties, and a heart burdened with sighs.

I look around at all I've seen,
The world outside, its beauty serene,
Yet, amidst the marvels, I'm adrift inside,
A stranger in a life I cannot divide.

I perceive myself through the eyes of others,
Mirroring back a hint of astonishment,
A face unknown, a tale untold,
A journey unfolding, young and old.

I reach out to touch the past,
Memories of laughter, love that will last,
Moments cherished, and tears that fell,
Echoes of moments that forever dwell.

My voice whispers secrets in the night,
As stars above shine with celestial light,
Their twinkling sparks ignite my soul,
Guiding me forward, making me whole.

At every step, a new path is made,
Each choice is a decision, not yet displayed,
A canvas waiting, black and white,
Awaiting brushstrokes of life's delight.

With every breath, a chance anew,
To redefine, rediscover, and breakthrough,
The boundaries of self, the chains that bind,
And find my true identity entwined.

Perhaps it's in the silence I'll hear,
The whispers of my heart, clear and dear,
Perhaps it's in the darkness I'll find,
The spark within was left behind.

For now, I'll wander, unanchored and wild,
Through labyrinths of who I used to be,
Until I stumble upon the truth I seek,
And find the answer to the question unique.

Who am I? A tale untold,
A chapter was written, as pages unfold,
A story spun, thread by thread,
Of trials and tribulations, joys and dread.

The more I search, the less I know,
The more I find, the more it grows,
Like a garden blooming, petals wide,
Unfurling layers, revealing my inside.

Perhaps it's in the journey I'll discover,
The answer lies in every moment I cover,
Maybe it's in the unknown, I'll find my way,
To the truth of who I am, come what may.

91

Harmony in Hushed Space: Finding My Voice

The stars that twinkled through the night,
Diminish from sight, like a fleeting light,
The moon's gentle glow no longer shines,
Leaving behind a peaceful dream that entwines.

In this serenity, I hear my voice,
A quiet truth, a sincere choice,
To let go of the noise and the strife,
And to welcome the stillness of life's light.

In that instant, I sense my heart's melody,
A rhythm that distinctly feels strong and free,
From the chaos of the world outside,
Where love and calm reside side by side.

The breeze shares whispers soft and mild,
Of distant peaks where eagles have filed,
Their shadows play against the sky's bright blue,
A symbol of freedom, bold and true.

In silence, I find my inner wisdom,
A gentle voice that prompts the next rhythm,
A spark within those shines so bright,
Illuminating darkness with its warm light.

With each breath, I sense myself awaken,
Like a lotus blossoming in peaceful, unshaken,
Petals spread, revealing beauty so rare,
A reflection of the soul, beyond compare.

Though the world may roar with noise and strife,
In the tranquillity, I discover my life,
A feeling of ease, a calm harbour,
Where love and wisdom forever wander.

In self-discovery, I chart my course,
Through the maze of each fleeting day's force,
A journey within, to my essence, truly,
Where love and light liberate uniquely.

The silence speaks, in a language so bright,
An orchestration of hope that dispels the fright,
A reminder that we're never alone,
Interwoven threads, in a fabric unknown.

In this serene time, I gather my might,
A resilience that aids me in flight,
The gap between who I once portrayed,
And who I'm becoming, wild and astray.

The quiet instructs, with a tender touch,
That growth and change start from such,
Where waves emerge, and ripples expand,
A narrative of transformation is still unplanned.

Let us treasure this peaceful domain,
This refuge where love does remain,
For in the hush, we find our sound,
A symphony that brings our hearts around.

92

Awakening Radiance: Threads of Hope Woven in Silence

The wise one of Arunachala, the light of dawn,
A profound question echoes, traversing the ages.
"Who am I?" he explored with earnest reflection,
Where latent truths in stillness lie, obscured from our sight.

Atma Vichara, the spark of self-inquiry,
Turning within, awakening the true essence.
Not merely inscribed on a charming surface,
But the core of existence, a priceless treasure.

The mind, a restless monkey, leaps and moves,
Grasping at forms, images, and chaos.
Allow thoughts to emerge, allow feelings to show,
But examine each one, "To whom do you belong, know?"

The "I-thought" surfaces, loud and self-assured,
The ego's hold, a narrative that observes.
Yet tracing back its delicate, fleeting thread,
To reveal the source within the heart's tranquil domain.

Dismantle identities, strip the layers away,
Beyond sensation, along the truest path.
Reject the false, the borrowed, and the superficial,
Until the Self, in solitude, continues to rule.

This inward journey, far from simple, calls,
Requires will, a yearning to be graced.
Persistence urged, a gentle, constant draw,
To reveal the peace that makes the broken whole.

For when the "I" fades in knowing light,
The separate self-yields to what is right.
The Atma glows, pure awareness unfettered,
The truth disclosed, on sacred, revered ground.

93

Cascades of Clarity: Ramana's Rhapsody for Restless Minds

In Tiruvannamalai's sacred hills so fair,
A sage did dwell, beyond compare,
Sri Ramana Maharshi, pure and bright,
Shone like the sun in morning light.

His eyes, like sapphires, deep and wide,
Reflected wisdom, side by side,
With compassion, love, and gentle might,
He guided seekers through the dark of night.

Born in 1879, in Tiruchuzhi land,
He wandered far, with a mystic hand,
Till Arunachala's peak he did abide,
And there his heart and soul did reside.

Arunachala's call, a whispered tone,
Summoned him forth, alone to atone,
To sit in silence, still and deep,
And find the Self, in endless sleep.

The world, with all its noise and fray,
Could not disturb his peaceful day,
For he had found the secret place,
Where love and truth did fill each space.

His teachings few, yet oh so grand,
Echoes of the infinite, in this land,
"Who am I?" the question he would ask,
And in the answer, all doubts do task.

The mind, a maze of thoughts so fast,
Must quiet down to pass the test,
Like lotus flowers, that bloom in the sea,
The ego's waves must set us free.

The Heart, a flame, that burns so bright,
Guides us home, through darkest night,
Through self-inquiry, we find our way,
To the still point, where love does stay.

Ramana's words, a balm to soothe,
Our souls, that wander, in life's truth,
His love, a shelter from life's stormy sea,
A refuge, where hearts can be free.

His presence, a gift from above,
A blessing, sent to endless love,
A shining star that guides us on,
Through the darkness, till the dawn is won.

The ashram, a haven, peaceful and still,
Where devotees gather to hear his will,
The silence, a mirror, reflects our soul,
In the depths of his loving goal.

The years went by, as he sat so tall,
Watching the world, with an all-seeing call,
His eyes, like windows, to the divine,
Reflected the beauty that is truly mine.

His passing left a void so wide,
Yet in our hearts, his spirit resides,
For in his teachings, we find our guide,
To the truth, that we cannot hide.

So, let us follow his path so bright,
And find our inner light,
For in his footsteps, we'll find our way,
To the Self, that shines, come what may.

In Tiruvannamalai's sacred hills so fair,
We'll remember Sri Ramana's care,
A sage, who showed us the way to be,
Free from suffering, wild and carefree.

In the annals of time and space,
His name, etched in love and praise,
A hero, a sage, a guiding light,
Sri Ramana Maharshi, shining bright.

94

Twilight Chronicles: The Enchantment of Night's Passage

Silence descends with the fading light,
A gentle caress that soothes the soul,
The stars begin their twinkling waltz tonight,
As day succumbs to the shadows' gentle role.

Moonbeams weave a silver tapestry so fine,
A celestial canvas, infinite and divine,
Night-blooming flowers sway to the breeze's sweet refrain,
Their petals dancing, a mesmerizing, ethereal strain.

In twilight's hush, where darkness softly falls,
The heart beats faster, with anticipation's thrall,
For in this realm of mystery and dreams untold,
Lies the promise of secrets yet to unfold.

The night air vibrates with whispers unspoken,
A symphony of whispers, hearts that have been broken,
Echoes of longing, yearning, love, and pain,
A melancholy serenade, an eternal refrain.

Yet, even as the shadows deepen and fears arise,
There's a beauty in this darkness, a hidden surprise,
A world of wonder waits, where magic reigns supreme,
And the unknown beckons, like a siren's mystic theme.

In this twilight realm, where reality blurs and fades,
The imagination knows no bounds, nor time constraints made.
The boundaries of dreams and fantasy entwine and blend,
As the night's dark canvas stretches out before us, a friend.

Like a lover's kiss, the wind caresses the trees,
Whispering ancient tales of long-forgotten ease,
The rustle of leaves, a language all its own,
A soothing melody that calms the restless bone.

In the stillness of the night, when the world is asleep,
I find solace, a peace that my soul can keep,
For in the darkness lies a light, a radiant glow,
A beacon guiding me through life's ebbs and flows.

95

The Dawn Dares Us:
The Dance Beyond Fear

In tranquil hills where silence reigns,
Arunachala beckons, shattering earthly chains.
A sage once roamed this blessed land,
With wisdom vast, a guiding presence is found.

Ramana, guardian of truth's soft light,
In every shadow, turned wrong to right.
He inspired stillness, the heart's deep song,
In the quiet depths, where we belong.

Here resides the essence, pure and bright,
The soul's authentic journey, beyond mere sight.
In meditative stillness, beneath this sky,
The mountain murmurs as time floats by.

Amidst paths of doubt and trails of fear,
His words are like balm, always near.
"Who am I? " Is the question that leads us home,
Within our hearts, we're never alone.

With each pulse, in every breath,
He showed the way through life and death.
A gentle spirit, wise and aware,
In the echoes of silence, love fills the air.

Underneath the stars, where shadows play,
The teachings persist, both night and day.
In the souls of those who seek, his light endures.
Arunachala Ramana, where the spirit thrives.

So here we place this humble stone,
A tribute to love, forever known.
In memory of a mentor, a friend so dear,
In the essence of truth, he is always near.

May we walk with courage, embrace the dawn,
With Ramana's wisdom, our fears are withdrawn.
In every sunrise, let us discover his grace.
Arunachala Ramana, our revered place.

96

A Tapestry of Forty-Two Threads: Woven for Sri Ramana Shiva

A young soul stirred, with death's presence so close,
Discovered the eternal Self, freeing him from the woes, Ramana
  Shiva.

To Arunachala, his hallowed mountain abode,
He attracted many seekers, guiding them down the road, Ramana
  Shiva.

The quiet mentor, with eyes that saw it all,
Responded to each query, answering every call, Ramana Shiva.

"Who am I?" the essence of his profound insight,
A journey to Self-realization, where truth takes flight, Ramana
  Shiva.

In tranquillity he lingered, a lighthouse of grace,
Steering wandering souls from darkness to a rightful place,
  Ramana Shiva.

His presence a blessing, a grace ever sincere,
Transforming the spirits of both many and few near, Ramana
  Shiva.

The illusion of ego, he encouraged us to discern,
Revealing the Atman, eternally unconfined, Ramana Shiva.

Words often unnecessary, his silence resounded clear,
Alleviating all uncertainties within the throngs gathered near,
Ramana Shiva.

Devotees encircled, embraced by his affection,
As their worldly bonds gradually faced rejection, Ramana Shiva.

The mountain his vessel, his breath the pure breeze,
His essence surrounding, beyond all to appease, Ramana Shiva.

Compassion incarnates, in thought, word, and action,
Sowing seeds of wisdom, fulfilling every fraction, Ramana Shiva.

The essence of reality, he articulated bright,
The Self as the origin, where all is intertwined, Ramana Shiva.

Through the practice of Self-inquiry, the 'I' thought ascends,
Unveiling the Self, the ultimate brilliance, Ramana Shiva.

His life stood as proof of truth's mighty hold,
Demonstrating the timeless, eternal path to behold, Ramana
Shiva.

The heart as the centre, where consciousness resides,
His teachings resonate, like sacred chimes that guide, Ramana
Shiva.

Transcending all dualities, he revealed the One,
Where division dissipates, and genuine peace is won, Ramana
Shiva.

His smile was a blessing, a calming release,
Bringing internal comfort, and profound inner peace, Ramana
Shiva.

The Master's embodiment, so simple yet grand,
To discover the Self, within this very land, Ramana Shiva.

His legacy continues, in hearts bright and pure,
A guiding star glowing, dispelling the obscure, Ramana Shiva.

The essence of Advaita, he clarified with ease,
The unity of all, dissolving every fear, Ramana Shiva.

Let us honour his art of wisdom so sweet,
And search for the true Self, residing where we meet, Ramana
Shiva.

97

Whispers of the Night Sky: Arunachala Under Moonbeams

A disc of silver, high above,
The full moon spills its gentle love.
On the sacred hill, a silent grace,
Arunachala, time and space.

The pilgrims gather, hearts alight,
Beneath the moon's ethereal light.
Barefoot steps on ancient ground,
A whispered prayer, without a sound.

The path unwinds, a cosmic thread,
Where shadows dance and stars are spread.
Each breath a mantra, soft and low,
Around the mountain, spirits flow.

The lunar glow, a guiding hand,
Across the mystical, hallowed land.
Reflecting peace, a tranquil scene,
Where earthly meets the ever-keen.

With every step, a deeper tie,
To the silent witness in the sky.
Full moon's blessing, pure and bright,
Embracing Arunachala's light.

The journey ends, the circle whole,
A quiet peace within the soul.
Bathed in moonlight, serene and deep,
The heart remembers secrets to keep.

98

Seeking Lord's Grace:
The Harmony of Hands Outstretched

In the stillness where the mountains breathe,
A sacred fire whispers through the night,
Arunachaleswarar, bold and luminous,
Enkindled spirit, in your light we weave.

Oh Lord of Flames, within this holy ground,
Your essence dances in each flickering spark;
From dim nooks to the dazzling arc,
In every heart's deep yearning, you are found.

The five great elements converge with grace—
Ether's elegance, Earth's steadfast embrace and water's flow,
Air's gentle caress and fire's fervent glow;
Yet among them all, your truth we trace.

Tiruvannamalai echoes a timeless song,
Where pilgrims tread on paths worn smooth by prayer;
With hands outstretched in reverence laid bare,
We lift our voices to join the throng.

As flames ascend toward heaven's vast expanse,
Each flicker tells of a love that will not cease;
In worship's fervour lies a perfect peace—
In accord with You—the eternal dance.

99

The Downward Gaze: Celestial Whirl of Nataraja's Grace

1. With tangled hair and a blazing crown aglow,
   He twirls forth, banishing the deepest woe.

2. A drum resounds, the rhythm of creation's call,
   The cosmos is encapsulated within its thrall.

3. His raised foot signifies a vow of liberation,
   From the cycles of birth, discovering true salvation.

4. An open hand extends, in Abhaya's tender grace,
   Offering comfort, in this hallowed place.

5. A flickering flame is cradled in another hand,
   The light of wisdom, illuminates the land.

6. His downward gaze, upon the demon laid to rest,
   Ignorance defeated; it might suppress.

7. A serpent winds, around his powerful arm,
   Kundalini's force, in its rightful charm.

8. He spirals and turns, in cosmic synchrony,
    A melody of joy, for all eternity.

9. The crescent moon graces his cascading hair,
    A representation of time, beyond compare.

10. His serene visage, a mask of pure bliss,
    As worlds emerge, and vanish into the abyss.

11. He is the origin, both beginning and end,
    The dance of existence, a cosmic blend.

12. In every movement, a universe awakens,
    His cosmic choreography, the tale of life has taken.

13. He embodies the dancer, the dance, and the platform,
    Turning the chapters, of life's sacred norm.

14. A timeless beat, found in his every stride,
    A cosmic performance, we can only abide.

15. He is Shiva, the annihilator and creator,
    The cosmic performer, the ultimate narrator.

16. His blissful dance, a vibrant, swirling creation,
    Capturing the essence of each pulsing sensation.

17. He spins and bounds, with limitless fervour,
    A showcase of elegance, for all to admire.

18. He reigns as lord of dance, Nataraja sublime,
    His cosmic essence will eternally shine.

19. He steps upon Apasmara, the dwarf of illusion's ties,
    Shattering the shackles of stories that rise.

20. His tangled hair, like the Ganga's flowing stream,
    Cleansing the universe, both above and beneath the dream.

21. He embodies the rhythm, the tune, and the verse,
    To which the cosmos has danced since the first.

100

Cascades of Affection: In Praise of Shiva's Sacred Heights

1. In silence, you rise, cloaked in ancient story,
   The heart of seekers, the pulse of glory, Arunachala Shiva.

2. Your rocks breathe wisdom, beneath the timeless firmament,
   A sacred whisper ever calling, never shy, Arunachala Shiva.

3. In the glow of dawn, your presence ignites,
   A dance of devotion in the soft morning light, Arunachala Shiva.

4. The river flows gently, reflecting your grace,
   In each ripple, a glimpse of your visage, Arunachala Shiva.

5. Pilgrims tread softly, drawn to your might,
   Seeking the truth in the stillness of the dark, Arunachala Shiva.

6. Clouds cradle your summit, a crown of white mist,
   In the heart of the heavens, where no soul can resist, Arunachala Shiva.

7. Mountains may tremble, yet you remain so grand,
   The anchor of my being, my all-in-all, Arunachala Shiva.

8. Through trials and tempest, you guide the wayfarer,
   A beacon of hope, no matter the cost, Arunachala Shiva.

9. In fiery sunsets, your colours unfold,
   Stories of existence, both timid and bold, Arunachala Shiva.

10. The night sky cradles a million bright dreams
    Under your watchful eye, everything redeems, Arunachala
    Shiva.

11. The stillness envelops, like a warm embrace,
    Here in your presence, I find my place, Arunachala Shiva.

12. With every prayer whispered, I draw near,
    Your sacred silence, all I long to hear, Arunachala Shiva.

13. The echoes of mantras in the cool evening air,
    A celestial chorus, transcending despair, Arunachala Shiva.

14. I walk the pathways, woven with grace,
    A journey of souls, in this timeless space, Arunachala Shiva.

15. As the stars wheel above, in a cosmic ballet,
    I release my ego, swaying in your luminescence, Arunachala
    Shiva.

16. Beneath your shadow, I shed all my fears,
    In the stillness of knowing, I find my tears, Arunachala Shiva.

17. Immovable fortress in a world of change,
    Your gaze is unwavering, forever arranged, Arunachala Shiva.

18. In the depth of my heart, your essence does thrive,
    The pulse of existence, the reason I strive, Arunachala Shiva.

19. In the dance of the flames, I see your reflection,
    A cycle of eternity, pure introspection, Arunachala Shiva.

20. Through laughter and sorrow, in joy or pain,
    Your grace is the answer, the light in the rain, Arunachala
    Shiva.

21. With every breath taken, a bond unconfined,
    I find my true self in the oneness of mind, Arunachala Shiva.

101

Choreography of Chaos:
The Divine Dance Unbound

In the stillness of night, where shadows entwine,
The cosmic drum echoes, a rhythm divine,
Lord Shiva, the dancer, in flames, takes his place,
A whirl of creation, a timeless embrace.

With trident held high, he conjures the storm.
Destruction and life in his tempestuous form,
From the ashes of worlds, new destinies spring.
In the dance of transformation, his praises we sing.

Beneath the crescent moon, his third eye aglow,
Illuminating truths that our heart longs to know,
With each cycle of time, the universe sways,
In the stillness of Shiva, eternity plays.

O Mahadev, in your silence profound,
In surrender, we find what true love has crowned.
Your presence, a guiding light, our spirits ignite,
In the depths of your being, we're one with the light.

102

Eight Notes of the Soul: Mindful Melodies to Sri Ramana

The Silent Sage

In the sanctuary of quietude, where tranquillity is found,
Sri Ramana Maharshi, your insights endure,
Within the stillness of awareness, the self-fades away.
In your tender embrace, the spirit grows.

The Light of Awareness

A guiding light in the turmoil of thoughts,
Through the veil of illusion, we seek your teachings.
"Who am I?" echoes a question profound,
In the depths of inquiry, our drowsiness, we shake off.

The Mountain of Grace

O Jewel of Arunachala, we stand in your light.
With grace flowing abundantly, like fine grains of sand,
Every step we take brings us nearer to you.
In the dance of existence, our souls are revitalized.

Beyond Words
In the sea of silence, where words cannot go,
You communicate with our spirits, where the mind is confused,
A truth that whispers, like the breeze through the leaves,
In your hallowed space, we discover complete peace.

Eternal Wisdom
Your gaze lifts the weight of grief and struggle,
In the simple yet profound, we reveal our existence.
The essence of life, so clear and expansive,
In the core of your teachings, our spirits find refuge.

The Path of Inquiry
O seer of the self, bathed in your grace,
You lead us inward to uncover our true essence,
With each layer uncovered, across the timeline,
The truth of our being, a harmony, resounds.

The Gift of Surrender
In the act of surrender, we uncover our authentic route to the
One.
With the flame of your wisdom, the journey begins.
As shadows softly fall and barriers begin to lift,
Through devotion and love, we awaken the heart.

Radiance of Being
Through the maelstrom of life, your presence endures.
A beacon of strength when the darkness recedes,
Sri Ramana Maharshi, in your essence we shine,
In the flow of existence, we move harmoniously together.

103

The Silent Choir of Arunachala: Five Songs from Beyond

Beacon of Light
In the cradle of dawn, where shadows meld,
Arunachala's silhouette, in silence held,
A source of brilliance, on the soul's barren shore,
Whispers of divinity — come forth, seek, explore.

A Reverent Heart
In the stillness of the night, under stars so bright,
The heart of Arunachala glows with a sacred light.
In every pulse of silence, in every touch of prayer,
Echoes the longing — O seeker, venture there.

The Call of the Mountain
O Mountain, sacred abode of the wise,
With gazes that pierce the veil 'neath the infinite skies.
To those who wander lost in the world's relentless race,
You are the refuge, the still, embracing grace.

Embrace of the Infinite
Layers of time melt in your eternal embrace,
With every step upward, I find my place.
The winds sing your glory, the stones hum your name,
In the heart of Arunachala, there's but one flame.

Sacred Oneness
Here in your presence, the self-fades away,
In the boundless ocean of love, where all shadows lay.
Arunachala, beloved, in your arms I reside,
In the timeless truth unveiled, the soul is our guide.

104

Illuminated by Firelight: Five Melodies from Arunachala's Peak

Lord of the Flames

O Arunachaleshwara, in your fiery might,
You shine like the sun, a guiding light.
You swirl within the flames of the cosmic order,
In the hearts of your followers, forever we honour.

Sacred Mountain's Lord

Beneath Arunachala, your presence is profound,
The resonance of your steps, in stillness abound.
With every breath we give, with each prayer we raise,
O Lord of the flame, in reverence we gaze.

Divine Compassion

Your gaze contains the wisdom of countless ages,
With love that ignites the tired and the cages.
Arunachaleshwara, bestow us your grace.
Lead us through the shadows in your warm embrace.

The Cosmic Dance

In the whirl of the universe, your energy flows,
O Lord of creation, in every heart glows.
Through life's challenges, your spirit we chase,
In the rhythm of devotion, we discover our place.

The Unfathomable

Beyond the formless void, where silence holds sway,
Arunachaleshwara, in you we lay.
The essence of all that exists always will be,
In your loving embrace, we find unity.

105

Whispers from Within: Five Threads on Mother Unnamulai's Tapestry

Mother of Grace
O Unnamulai, cherished mother so dear,
In your loving arms, all troubles disappear.
With a heart brimming with kindness, your love discloses,
In the solace of your presence, we find our purpose.

Guardian of Souls
Beneath the sacred skies, where your gifts flow unbounded,
O Mother, in your glow we thrive, surrounded.
Through struggles and darkness, you lead us each hour.
In the rhythm of devotion, we find our power.

The Healing Touch
With a soft murmur of kindness that eases every pain,
O Mother, like the gentlest rain.
You carry our grief, filling us with grace,
In the love-infused garden, we flourish in this space.

The Eternal Light

In the sacred glow of your endless love,
O Mother, unwavering, reflecting from above.
The stars in their courses, the moon on her flight,
All resonate, your majesty, our beacon of light.

The Divine Embrace

As we unite in reverence beneath the hallowed trees,
O Mother, we feel your gentle breeze.
With every open heart, your blessings cascade.
In the harmony of spirit, our souls you upgrade.

106

Hum Beneath the Heights: Arunachala's Veiled Vigour

Silent.
A mountain breathes.
Not of wind,
But of Being.

Ramana.
A name,
A stillness.

Who am I?
The question,
A razor's edge,
Peeling back layers of
Dust,
Illusion,
Story.

The cave,
A womb.
Birth inward.

No guru,
Only pointing.
A finger
Moonward.

Atman.
The self,
Unbound,
Unnamed.
The gaze,
Unwavering,
A pool
Reflecting
Sky.

Words fall away.
Like autumn leaves,
Returning to
Root.

Silence roars.
Arunachala's hum
Vibrates
In the chest.

Be Still.

The heart
A hollow gourd,
Filled
With the
Unborn.

Ramana.
Not a person,
But a space.
An invitation,
To dissolve.

No path,
Only presence.

I AM.

107

In the Shadow of Wisdom: Five Hymns on the One Who Faces the South

The Silent Teacher
O Dakshinamoorthy, in stillness you abide,
With wisdom as profound as the ocean's tide.
In a noisy world, your serenity is a balm,
Through the tranquillity of your eyes, we confront our qualm.

Master of the Universe
Beneath the sacred banyan, your essence radiates,
O Lord of all seekers, you banish the dark.
With a hand uplifted in blessing and eyes filled with kindness,
Within the depths of your wisdom, we find our true place.

The Journey of Enlightenment
O Dakshinamoorthy, lead us on our way,
In the search for truth, we find where we stay.
With every soft lesson, each moment you weave,
In the tapestry of knowledge, our spirits believe.

The Light of Understanding

With the flame of your insight, kindle the divine,

O Lord of scholars, in our souls let you shine.

Through the darkness of ignorance, your brilliance we chase,

In the domain of enlightenment, we merge with your grace.

The Unfathomable Depth

Within the depths of your essence, great truths lie,

O Dakshinamoorthy, our constant guide and ally.

With your peaceful presence, we let go of our dread.

In the warmth of your light, transcending all that's said.

108

The Final Benediction:
A Symphony of Final Strokes

Sri Maha Ganapati, we bow to Thee.
With humble hearts and bend knees.
We seek Thy guidance in this worldly strife,
To lead us safely through the path of life.
Shield us from the darkness and the fear,
And hold us close throughout the passing year.
Grant us the wisdom to discern the truth,
And fill our hearts with everlasting youth.
Bestow upon us the strength to overcome,
The challenges that make our spirits numb.
Inspire us to create, to love, to learn,
And may our inner fire brightly burn.
May all beings everywhere find peace.
And may the cycle of suffering cease.
May all find solace in your tender grace,
And may we all behold your loving face
Gajanana, our Lord Divine,
Your blessings shower, eternally shine.

This epic end, a humble offering made,
In gratitude and love, forever stayed.
The invocation complete, the verses cease,
Leaving behind a sense of profound calmness and peace.

Om!

Glossary

A

Advaita

A philosophical concept meaning "non-dualism," Advaita is often associated with the teachings of Dakshinamoorthy. It posits that the individual self (Atman) and the ultimate reality (Brahman) are one and the same, emphasizing the importance of realizing this unity for spiritual awakening.

Agni Lingam

The Agni Lingam, or Fire Lingam, symbolizes the element of fire in Hindu philosophy. It represents transformation, energy, and purification. Often associated with the deity Shiva, this lingam is revered in rituals aimed at igniting passion and creativity in one's life. Imagine standing before a flickering flame, feeling its warmth and vibrant energy—this is the essence of the Agni Lingam.

Apasmara

This is a fascinating figure from Hindu mythology, often depicted as a dwarf demon. He symbolizes ignorance and is known for trying to distract and mislead spiritual seekers. In a way, he represents those nagging doubts or distractions we all face on our journey toward enlightenment—like that little voice in your head that says, "You can't do this!"

Arunachala

A sacred hill in South India, revered as a manifestation of Lord Shiva. It's seen as a place of deep spiritual significance, representing both a physical and a metaphorical journey toward enlightenment and self-discovery.

Arunachaleshwarar

Arunachaleshwarar is a revered deity in Hinduism, particularly within the Shaivism tradition. He is worshipped as a form of Lord Shiva and is intimately connected to the sacred hill of Arunachala in Tamil Nadu, India. Devotees believe that this divine form embodies the essence of fire and represents the ultimate truth, guiding seekers on their spiritual journey.

Arunagiri

The term "Arunagiri" refers to the sacred hill of Arunachala, which holds immense spiritual significance in Hinduism. Often seen as a manifestation of Lord Shiva, this hill is a pilgrimage site where devotees seek enlightenment and liberation. The serene environment and rich spiritual history of Arunagiri make it a cherished destination for those on a quest for inner peace and divine connection.

Arunagiri Nadar

Arunagiri Nadar was a prominent Tamil poet and saint, celebrated for his devotional hymns dedicated to Lord Murugan, the son of Lord Shiva. His works, including the famous "Tiruppugazh," are known for their lyrical beauty and deep spiritual insight. Arunagiri Nadar's life and poetry inspire countless devotees, emphasizing the power of devotion and the transformative nature of love for the divine.

Ardhanarishwarar

A divine representation in Hindu mythology, symbolizing the union of the Lord Shiva and Goddess Parvati. This form embodies the balance of masculine and feminine energies, illustrating the interdependence of opposites in the universe.

Annamalaiyar Temple

This is the big, beautiful temple dedicated to Lord Shiva right in the heart of Tiruvannamalai. It's not just a place of worship; it's like a vibrant community center where locals and visitors come together to soak in the spirituality and culture. You'll often see people strolling around, taking in the stunning architecture and the peaceful vibes.

Azhagammal

Azhagammal was the mother of Sri Ramana Maharishi. Her nurturing and compassionate nature played a crucial role in shaping the early life of Ramana. She is often remembered for her unconditional love and support, which fostered his spiritual journey.

B

Bhairava

Bhairava is a fierce manifestation of Lord Shiva, often depicted as a protector and guardian of time and space. He embodies the concept of absolute reality and is revered as the deity who helps devotees overcome their fears and obstacles. In many traditions, he is seen as a guide through life's challenges, encouraging individuals to embrace change and transformation.

Brahma

Brahma is known as the creator god in Hindu mythology. Think of him as the ultimate architect of the universe! He's part of the Trimurti, which includes Vishnu and Shiva, and while he might not get as much attention in modern stories, he's crucial for kicking off the whole cosmic drama.

Buddhipriya

A term that translates to "Beloved of Wisdom." It highlights the connection between Lord Ganesha and the pursuit of knowledge and understanding, appealing to those who seek clarity and insight in their lives.

D

Dakshinamoorthy:

A revered form of Lord Shiva, depicted as a guru or teacher, symbolizing wisdom and knowledge. The term "Dakshina" means south, and "Moorthy" refers to the form or deity. This representation emphasizes the importance of imparting spiritual wisdom to seekers.

E

Ego

The sense of self that often identifies with thoughts, emotions, and external circumstances. In spiritual contexts, the ego is seen as a barrier to true understanding and connection with the self, often creating illusions that lead to suffering.

Esanya Lingam

Esanya Lingam is linked to the northeast direction and represents the divine energy of Lord Shiva in this aspect. It is revered for its spiritual significance, as it symbolizes knowledge, wisdom, and the pursuit of enlightenment. Many come here seeking inner peace and a deeper understanding of themselves.

G

Gajanana

A name for Lord Ganesha, often depicted with the head of an elephant. He's known as the remover of obstacles and the deity of wisdom and beginnings. In the context of the poem, he symbolizes guidance and inspiration.

Ganesha

A beloved deity in Hinduism, Ganesha is the elephant-headed God known as the remover of obstacles and the god of beginnings. He's often called upon for guidance in new endeavors, reflecting the importance of starting fresh and overcoming challenges in life.

Ghee

A type of clarified butter originating from Indian cuisine, ghee is made by simmering butter to remove moisture and milk solids. This process results in a rich, golden oil with a nutty flavor and a high smoke point, making it ideal for cooking. Beyond its culinary uses, ghee holds deep spiritual significance in various cultures, often associated with purity, health, and sacred rituals.

Girivalam

This is the ritual circumambulation of Arunachala, where devotees walk around the mountain, usually around 14 kilometers. It's not just exercise; it's a meditative journey for many, allowing them to reflect and connect deeply with their spiritual selves. The atmosphere is filled with devotion and serenity.

I

Indra Lingam

Indra Lingam represents the god Indra, known as the king of the heavens in Hindu mythology. This lingam symbolizes power, authority, and the vital connection between the earthly realm and the divine. Pilgrims visit this lingam to seek strength and protection in their lives.

K

Karthigai Deepam

Karthigai Deepam is an important festival celebrated in Tiruvannamalai, typically in November or December. It involves lighting lamps and a massive fire atop Arunachala Hill, symbolizing the light of consciousness. This festival draws thousands of devotees, creating a vibrant atmosphere filled with devotion and celebration.

Ketaki Flower

A flower often associated with purity and truth in Hindu mythology. In the poem, it becomes a symbol of deceit when Brahma uses it to falsely claim victory, highlighting how appearances can be misleading and the consequences of dishonesty.

Kubera Lingam

Kubera Lingam is dedicated to Kubera, the god of wealth and prosperity. This lingam is a popular destination for those desiring material abundance and financial stability. Devotees pray here to attract prosperity and to express gratitude for the blessings they receive in life.

L

Lambodara

This term refers to one of the forms of Lord Ganesha, who is often depicted with a large belly. The name literally means "one with a big belly," symbolizing abundance and the ability to digest all of life's experiences, good and bad. Ganesha is commonly worshipped at the start of new ventures for blessings and success.

Lingam

A representation of Lord Shiva, often symbolizing the universe and creation. It's a powerful emblem in spiritual practices, evoking the idea of deeper truths and cosmic energy, encouraging us to explore the unseen aspects of existence.

M

Madurai

Madurai is a historic city in Tamil Nadu, situated not far from Tiruchuli. Known for its rich cultural heritage and the magnificent Meenakshi Amman Temple, Madurai serves as a backdrop to the early life of Ramana Maharishi. The city symbolizes the confluence of spirituality and tradition, echoing the values and teachings that Ramana eventually embodied.

Maharishi

A title of respect in Hindu culture, often translated as "great sage" or "great seer." It is commonly associated with spiritual leaders and teachers who possess profound wisdom and insight into the nature of reality and consciousness.

Mantra

A word or phrase, often repeated during meditation, intended to focus the mind and create a sense of inner peace. Mantras can be personal or traditional, like OM, and are tools for calming the spirit and alleviating fears, helping us tap into deeper states of awareness.

Meditative Tranquillity

A state of calm achieved during meditation, where one can experience deep peace and connection with the self and the universe. It's that serene place where distractions fade, allowing for introspection and the discovery of the innate rhythms within each of us.

Meditation

A practice that involves focusing the mind and eliminating distractions to achieve a state of deep relaxation and heightened awareness. It's often seen as a way to connect with the divine or gain insights into life's mysteries.

N

Nataraja

Nataraja, often referred to as the "Lord of Dance," is a form of the Hindu god Shiva. This representation embodies the cosmic cycles of creation and destruction, symbolizing the rhythmic nature of the universe. His dance, known as the Tandava, reflects the balance of creation and dissolution, showcasing the divine play of existence.

Niruthi Lingam

Niruthi Lingam is a sacred representation of Lord Shiva, particularly revered in the context of the Tiruvannamalai temple. It symbolizes the direction of the south in Hindu cosmology and is associated with the removal of obstacles and the dispelling of negative energies.

O

OM

A sacred syllable in many spiritual traditions, OM represents the essence of the universe. It's seen as the sound of creation, embodying everything from the tiniest atom to the vast cosmos. When chanted, it's said to connect us to the very fabric of existence, bringing peace and clarity to the mind.

P

Parvati

Parvati is a prominent goddess in Hindu mythology, known as the wife of Lord Shiva and the mother of Lord Ganesha and Lord Kartikeya. She embodies love, devotion, and fertility, symbolizing the nurturing aspects of femininity and the balance between strength and compassion.

Pichandavar

Pichandavar is a lesser-known deity associated with the worship of Kala Bhairava. He is often revered as the one who grants wisdom and knowledge, guiding devotees toward enlightenment. His name reflects a specific aspect of divine power, emphasizing his role in the spiritual journey of individuals seeking deeper understanding and clarity.

Primordial Hum

The ancient, foundational sound that existed before anything else. It's often described as a deep, resonant vibration from which all forms of energy and existence arise. Think of it as the universe's heartbeat, quietly pulsing through everything.

Pradakshina

This is the act of walking in a clockwise circle around a sacred object or place, often done in a spiritual or religious context. Think of it as a way to honor and connect with something deeply meaningful—like walking around a beloved tree or a special shrine, feeling that energy envelop you.

R

Ramana Maharshi

A revered Indian sage born in 1879, known for his teachings on self-realization and the practice of self-inquiry. His approach emphasizes the importance of looking within to discover one's true nature and understanding the self beyond the ego.

S

Self-inquiry

A contemplative practice where individuals explore the question "Who am I?" to uncover their true essence beyond thoughts and ego. This introspective method is designed to peel away layers of identity and reveal the deeper self that lies within.

Self-Realization

Self-realization refers to the profound understanding and awareness of one's true nature, which transcends the ego and the physical self. For Sri Ramana Maharishi, this journey inward leads to the recognition that our essence is pure consciousness, a state of being that brings lasting peace and clarity.

Shakti

Shakti refers to the divine feminine energy believed to be the source of all creation and power in the universe. In the context of Goddess Parvati, Shakti represents her strength and ability to inspire and empower others, highlighting her role as a protector and nurturer.

Shiva

In Hinduism, Shiva is one of the principal deities, often known as the destroyer and transformer within the Trimurti, which also includes Brahma the creator and Vishnu the preserver. He embodies paradoxes, being both fierce and gentle, and is often depicted in a meditative state.

Skandasramam

Skandasramam is an ashram located on the sacred Arunachala, founded by Sri Ramana Maharishi. This tranquil retreat is significant for spiritual seekers, offering a space for meditation, reflection, and self-inquiry. The ashram serves as a reminder of Maharishi's teachings, encouraging visitors to delve deep into their own consciousness and explore the essence of existence.

Sonagiri

A revered name for Arunachala Hill, often associated with spiritual significance and devotion. The term reflects the hill's rich cultural heritage and its role as a pilgrimage site for many seeking spiritual enlightenment.

Sri Ramanasramam

A spiritual retreat located in Tiruvannamalai, India, founded by the renowned Indian sage Sri Ramana Maharshi. It serves as a place for seekers of truth to engage in self-inquiry and meditation, fostering a deep connection to the teachings of Ramana Maharshi.

Surya Lingam

The Surya Lingam represents the sun and its life-giving energy. Associated with health, vitality, and illumination, this lingam is often venerated for its ability to dispel darkness and negativity. Picture a bright, sunny day that uplifts your spirits—this is the power of the Surya Lingam, encouraging us to embrace positivity and radiate warmth in our lives.

T

Tandava

The Tandava is a vigorous dance that is said to be performed by Lord Shiva, representing the cosmic cycles of creation, preservation, and dissolution. It embodies both the destructive and creative aspects of the universe, highlighting the duality inherent in life itself. This dance is not only a form of expression but also a cosmic energy that influences the rhythm of the universe.

Tiruchuli

Tiruchuli is a small town located in the Virudhunagar district of Tamil Nadu, India. It holds significant spiritual importance as it is recognized as the birthplace of Sri Ramana Maharishi, a revered figure in Indian spirituality. The town is not just a geographical location; it embodies a deep sense of devotion and tranquility, reflecting the essence of Ramana Maharishi's teachings.

Tiruvannamalai

Tiruvannamalai is a town in Tamil Nadu famous for its sacred mountain, Arunachala, which is considered a manifestation of Lord Shiva. This town serves as a spiritual center, drawing seekers from around the world for its unique blend of culture, spirituality, and natural beauty.

U

Unnamulai

The divine goddess worshiped in the temple at Tiruvannamalai. She embodies compassion and grace, welcoming devotees with open arms, symbolizing protection and strength in times of need.

V

Varuna Lingam

The Varuna Lingam embodies the element of water. It signifies fluidity, adaptability, and emotional depth. In Hindu mythology, Varuna is the god of water and cosmic order, and the Varuna Lingam serves as a reminder of the importance of balance in life. Just as water flows and nourishes, this lingam encourages us to embrace change and find harmony within ourselves and our surroundings.

Vayu Lingam

Vayu Lingam is associated with Vayu, the god of wind. This lingam embodies the essential force of life and movement. Visitors to Vayu Lingam often seek clarity and guidance, hoping to harness the dynamic energy of wind to propel them forward in their spiritual journeys.

Vignaharta

A title for Lord Ganesha, meaning "the remover of obstacles." This term emphasizes his role in helping devotees overcome challenges on their spiritual paths, making it relatable for anyone facing difficulties in life.

Vishnu

Vishnu is often seen as the preserver of the universe. If Brahma is the architect, then Vishnu is the one who maintains everything— like a diligent property manager making sure everything runs smoothly. He has a ton of avatars (like Krishna and Rama) that he takes on to restore balance and protect dharma (moral order).

Y

Yama Lingam

Yama Lingam is dedicated to Yama, the god of death and dharma. This lingam serves as a reminder of the transient nature of life and the importance of living righteously. Devotees often pray here for a peaceful journey in the afterlife and to honor their ancestors.